Teaching Martial Arts

A Practical Guide

Copyright © 2009 Bill Pottle and Katie Hoffman

ISBN 978-1-60145-935-0

All rights reserved. No part of this publication may be reproduced, stored in a retrieval system, or transmitted in any form or by any means, electronic, mechanical, recording or otherwise, without the prior written permission of the author.

Printed in the United States of America.

Disclaimer

This book is intended to provide only general information about key concepts and theories related to the instruction of martial arts. No part of it should be construed as offering any legal, medical, or professional advice. The reader assumes all risk of injury, lawsuit, or other loss resulting from the use of any part of this book. Consult a physician before beginning any exercise program. Consult with relevant professionals who are skilled in the legal systems of your locality before making any changes to your martial arts program.

Booklocker.com, Inc.
2009

Teaching Martial Arts
A Practical Guide

Bill Pottle and Katie Hoffman

Acknowledgments

We want to thank all of the people who helped make this work possible. Our instructors, Master Ghassan Timani and Master Han Cho, helped us gain insight into the world of martial arts instruction. Dr. Mike Burson served as medical advisor to the work. Evan Kramer helped with diagrams and proofreading. We especially owe a big thank you to the entire KAT instructor training class which worked so diligently preparing and discussing these lessons.

Medical Advisor's Statement

It was an honor and privilege to have been provided the opportunity to review this instructor manual for Master Pottle. As a physician, I appreciate the challenge of explaining a difficult subject such as anatomy and physiology in such a way as to make it understandable and meaningful to a wide student population. Master Pottle has succeeded in this effort with this manual. Additionally, as a student of Taekwondo, I appreciate the practical aspect of this topic. Throughout this manual Master Pottle incorporates basic science with the study of Taekwondo, resulting in a complete, practical, integrated resource for any instructor.

Michael Burson, MD PhD
Physician and Black Belt

Basic Lessons

About This Book and How to Use It xi
Lesson 1: Student/Teacher Relationship. 1
Lesson 2: Fundamental Concepts and Leadership Skills 4
Lesson 3: Ten Influential Martial Artists 10
Lesson 4: Communication Skills 16
Lesson 5: Learning Styles 18
Lesson 6: Personality Types 20
Lesson 7: Teaching Techniques 23
Lesson 8: General Training Effects 30
Lesson 9: The Ideal Class 32
Lesson 10: Student Retention 34
Lesson 11: Safety First 40
Lesson 12: Warm-ups 42
Lesson 13: Basics and Traditional Techniques 45
Lesson 14: Paddle Drills 48
Lesson 15: Partner Drills 50
Lesson 16: Promotion Tests 53
Lesson 17: One Step Sparring 54
Lesson 18: Teaching Forms 56
Lesson 19: Teaching Sport Combat (Grappling and Sparring) 59
Lesson 20: Teaching Combat 66
Lesson 21: Teaching Non-Physical Requirements 68
Lesson 22: Classroom Management 71
Lesson 23: Games 73
Lesson 24: Special Students 81
Lesson 25: Discipline and Punishment 85
Lesson 26: Legal Issues 90

Lesson 27: Parents 94
Lesson 28: Body Planes and Motions 97
Lesson 29: Physiology of Training 100
Lesson 30: Foot and Ankle 103
Lesson 31: Shin and Knee 106
Lesson 32: Hip 110
Lesson 33: Core 112
Lesson 34: Spine 115
Lesson 35: Shoulder 118
Lesson 36: Hand and Arm 120
Lesson 37: The Eye 123
Lesson 38: The Ear 126
Lesson 39: Nervous System 130
Lesson 40: Immune System 133
Lesson 41: Muscle System 137
Lesson 42: Combining Forms 140
Lesson 43: Curriculum Design 151
Lesson 44: Basic Business Concepts 153
Lesson 45: Coaching at Tournaments 155
Lesson 46: Basic Physics of Martial Arts 157
Class Planning Worksheet 164
Class Report 165
The Misadventures of Master Malo: Class 166
Master Malo and The Promotion Test 168
Master Malo Goes to the Tournament 171
Sample Certification Requirements 176
References 178

About This Book and How to Use It

This book was written to consolidate the lessons of the instructor training course of the Korean Academy of Taekwondo (www.kattaekwondo.com) and then generalized to be of use to other martial arts schools. This book can be read by beginning or experienced instructors to provide insight into aspects of teaching martial arts.

This book is divided into lessons, each dealing with a specific aspect of martial arts pedagogy. Each lesson can be read as a chapter or used by the head instructor for teaching that concept in an instructor training or leadership skills course. At www.martial-arts-instructor-training.com, you can find more resources as well as quizzes for each lesson that can be given out by hand or over the internet to ensure that students understand the material. The above website also has tests that can be given to certify students at each of the levels of instructor competency decided on by your school. Please see the sample certification requirements in the back of the book for an idea.

There is a companion site to this book, www.wikidrills.com, which features videos, pictures, and descriptions of different martial arts drills that you can use in your classroom. The site is in wiki format so people from all over the world can contribute their knowledge and experience.

Job Description: The successful applicant will be required to perform the tasks of all of the following professions.

Child Development Specialist
Safety Inspector and Implementation Expert
Skills Transfer Optimization Engineer
Combat Readiness Trainer
Historical Artifact Curator
Cultural Anthropological Communication Service Provider
First Responder for Medical Emergencies
Behavior Adaptation Specialist
Interior Decorator
Biophysicist
Nutritionist
Marketing and Sales Professional
Preschool – Senior Citizen Psychologist
Success Coach
Dispute Mediator
Motivational Speaker
Tamer of Large Mammals
Communication Facilitator
Strategic Consultant
Press Secretary
Image Consultant
Drill Sergeant
Grief Counselor
Public Speaker
Marriage Counselor
Confidant
Biohazardous Waste Disposal Expert
Digital Video Analyzer
Community Service Volunteer
… and Role Model.

…And they could have just said – Martial Arts Instructor.

If it seems like a lot of tasks- it is. This course will help you to understand many of the things you will be doing in your career as a martial arts instructor. As always, there is no substitute for experience, but this course should help you get well on your way to getting there.

It's important to know that as a martial arts instructor, you will probably be the most influential person in the lives of some of your students. Ideally, parents should be more of an influence, but this is not always the case. In this age of divorced parents, you may be the only male (or female) role model in a child's life. Even with adult students, they may have lost their parents or have few friends outside of the school. School teachers see the children Monday through Friday, for many hours each day, but only see them for a year, whereas you may see them for several years, even decades. This is a very humbling thought. You have a prodigious responsibility. Yet, if this is not enough, consider that if you teach the student well and he also uses the lessons learned from this program, he will go on to influence many people. If you teach 100 people well and they teach 100 people, now there are 10,000 people living a better life. Conversely, if you teach things poorly, the result will be the opposite. One instructor has a tremendous potential to effect good or evil in the world.

You will teach people much more than you intend to. They will look at your life, at your personal relationships, at your tone of voice. They will notice your body language. They will subconsciously become more like you. If you can't handle that, then you have no business being a martial arts instructor.

If you have no moral or value system, your students may believe that there is no such thing as right or wrong. Without morality and a framework for the techniques, all you really will do is create more powerful bullies.

The seeds of countless great classes are hidden within each of you. The only limit to what you can accomplish is your own drive and creativity.

"You can get whatever you want in life, if you help enough other people get what they want." Zig Ziglar.

Lesson 1: Student/Teacher Relationship.

The relationship between the students and their instructor or master is critically important. If you are an assistant instructor, your relationship will not be the same as if you are the head instructor in the school. However, your relationships will still have some of the same elements.

When purchasing the KAT school from my instructor, I asked him what he would miss most about owning the school. He did not have to think long to say that it would be the relationships that he had developed over the years with his students. While we treasure these relationships over other gains we get from teaching, there are many pitfalls that must be avoided. Your students are your customers. They need to be treated well like other customers are (i.e., given more value than they receive) but should not be treated only as customers. They are your friends, but can't be treated just like a friend. Your relationship is not the same as a public school teacher, nor is it the same as with other customers. If a small hardware store owner needed to go on vacation, he wouldn't ask his customers to come in and run the registers while he was gone, but many of your students would love to do the same for you.

Sadly, in the past this relationship has led to much abuse from both sides. Masters have asked way too much from their trusting students, who have also treated their instructors badly. Masters have traded rank for sex or money, or even tried to become cult-like figures. Here are a few common sense limits on your relationship with your students.

- **Religious Issues** – Certainly, your students will come to know and respect your worldview, and this will influence their thinking. It would probably not be improper to invite a student, especially one without a religion and looking for one, to come worship with you. However, actively trying to convert students, especially children, is over the line. This type of behavior will definitely not be appreciated. The exception of course is if you are a specific type of martial arts school, and that is made clear. For instance, a Christian Martial Arts school would be justified in praying together out loud before class. One of our instructors runs a program in a Mosque, and the students there stop class whenever it is time to pray and resume training later.

- **Medical or Legal Issues** – Of course, students will come to you for advice about everything. However, unless you're a doctor or a lawyer, you should always recommend seeing one. In the worst case scenario, you could be accused of practicing medicine or law without a license. Use common sense. Telling a student to ice a bruise is fine, trying to set his broken bone is not. Giving a student advice about a legal matter might be okay, as long as he understands that you are not an expert in that area of law and that your advice is nothing more than the opinion of a friend.

The danger is that because martial arts instructors have to be experts at so many things, our students may come to believe that we are experts at everything, and we may come to believe this as well. You wouldn't want a computer programmer to tell you how to teach any more than a programmer would want you to tell him how to program.

Although the Student/Teacher relationship is not one of the five main Confucian relationships, it draws heavily on Asian culture and Confucian thought. At the lowest level, the relationship can be thought of as the student will do whatever the master says, and the master will teach martial arts as he has been taught. However, there are many important subtleties in the relationship that are overlooked.

- **Master's Responsibilities** – The master is responsible for teaching the student more than just technique. He must also put that technique in a moral framework. The master is also responsible for taking care of a student outside of the framework of a class. He should ensure the student can use the lessons of training to make his life better. A master fails if his student flunks out of academic school, no matter how good he is at martial arts technique. A master should help his student achieve his potential in life, and also teach his top students how to teach what they have been taught.

    The master's responsibility is also to protect the students from physical and emotional harm. In a real self defense situation, he should be ready and able to protect them. Though a situation might be emotionally painful for him, he must put his students' needs above his own.

The master himself must be an example of the benefits of training. If he teaches discipline, he must be disciplined. He must be in good shape, and he must always train. The master shouldn't ask students to do things he won't do. Of course, this doesn't mean that if he can only do a 540 kick, he shouldn't get students to do a 720. **The ultimate goal of a master is to raise students who are better than he is.** It means that you can't tell people to do things without supporting them. It's probably not possible to train 18 hours a day, and you can't ask your students to do that, especially if you never have. If you demand sacrifice from your students, you have to sacrifice too.

- **Student's Responsibilities** – The student has to listen to what the master says and do it without questioning. This doesn't mean that students shouldn't think, but that they must trust that there is a reason they need to paint the fence or wax on/wax off. They need to trust the master's experience. The student should respect the master and the rules of the school.

  A student should show up on time, ready to work hard. The other main responsibility of the student is to pay his tuition, which is what keeps the school going.

It should be noted that although the student pays the master, the student can never fully pay the master back until the student has students of his own. This is analogous to the parent/child relationship. Even though you might take care of your parents when they are older, there is no way that you can ever really repay them for all those diapers they changed of yours when you were little, or all the things that they sacrificed for you. You can really only fulfill your debt to your parents by raising your own children right.

You do not have to follow the traditional relationship model, and each person will develop a relationship based on your personality and the personalities of your students. However, this is a model that has worked for many generations of students and teachers, and will work for many more.

Treasure the relationships you have with your students, as they will be some of the most precious rewards you ever receive from your long hours of work as a martial arts instructor.

Lesson 2: Fundamental Concepts and Leadership Skills

Leadership

Leadership is one of the most important qualities that an instructor must possess. A leader will be able to get other people to follow him. Without leadership, we cannot inspire our students to follow us and we will not be able to impact positive changes in their lives. Don't ask to be a leader. Just lead, in every way possible. People will follow you.

"*A leader is a dealer in hope.*" - **Napoleon**

What makes a good leader has been the subject of numerous debates for many years. Every year hundreds of business books are published on the subject, covering a wide range of ideas and styles. Machiavelli's *The Prince* (1532) posited that leaders should be ruthless, pragmatic, and decisive. He believed that it was better to be feared than to be loved. We also have modern books that embrace a "touchy –feely" approach to leadership. What is the best way for us as martial artists to be leaders?

In 1939, psychologist Kurt Lewin's team published their research that identified three specific leadership styles.

Authoritarian – Authoritarian leaders provide clear expectations on what to do, how to do it, and when it should be done. There is a clear division between who is giving the orders and who is following them. Students are productive under this style of leadership, but can lack creativity.

Democratic – Democratic leaders take input from others before making decisions. When presented with a question, they will vote to see how each person is feeling. The will of the majority is more important than the ideas of the leader. Students are less productive here, but what they produce is creative and of high quality.

Delegative – These types of leaders have a "hands off" approach, giving the people under them the power to make decisions and take action based on those decisions. Students are least productive here, and also complain the most.

Many people probably consider martial arts teachers to lead with an authoritarian style, but in reality, the best leaders will use different styles at different points. Authoritative leadership is better when the students have little knowledge, while delegative can be good when others have a higher skill. For instance, you wouldn't want to let the white belts choose what to do in class (democratic) because they are just beginners and do not know how to do the various drills required. However, you will eventually want to delegate teaching part or all of a class to your senior students and other instructors. Understanding these styles and the benefits and deficiencies of each can help you to use the right style for the right situation.

Here are several qualities that a leader should possess:

- **Vision** – A leader absolutely must be able to see things that do not yet exist and develop a plan to get there. A leader must be able to set specific, measurable goals and inspire others to help him reach them. A leader without a vision is like a fly buzzing around the room aimlessly. You might lead people, but they won't get anywhere special.

- **The Ability to Inspire** – As the above quote suggests, a leader should inspire people to be able to hope for something better.

- **Responsibility** – The person at the top always has to take responsibility for what happens in his class/school/company.
    - When good things come, leaders should credit the people below them who helped make it all possible.
    - When bad things come, leaders should take the blame themselves and take steps to fix the problem or make sure it never happens again.

- **A Mentor** – Great leaders need mentors as well. These people can help teach about how to be a leader. Even the President and the Pope have leaders that they look up to. When you think you're going through difficult times, there's probably someone else out there who has already passed through that.

- **A Focus on Solutions Instead of Problems** – Losers will think about the problems that exist and use them as an excuse for why they fail. Winners will spend their time thinking about solutions and create a path to success no matter what the situation.

- **The Ability to Act Decisively and Take Risks** – Sometimes leaders must make decisions and act, even without perfect information. While it's never a good idea to do things without thinking, sometimes leaders need to be able to cut off the discussions and just act. Imagine when several friends get together and try to figure out where to go to dinner. Sometimes, someone needs to just say what is happening to avoid a 45 minute discussion on it.

Keep in mind that leadership skills can be used for positive or negative ends. Many of history's greatest villains have also been great leaders. They just used their abilities to cause pain and suffering to an unimaginable number of people.

Benefits of Martial Arts

By now you should have seen many benefits of training in your own life and the lives of your friends and teammates. Here is another list of the benefits of training:

Key Physical Benefits

- Improved cardiovascular health and endurance
- Improved strength and muscle tone
- Sustainable weight loss
- Improved agility and coordination
- Ability to defend yourself or others

Key Psychological Benefits

- Self confidence
- Discipline
- Ability to perform under pressure

- Ability to work together as a part of a team
- Ability to work towards a difficult but attainable goal

<u>Key Mental Benefits</u>

- Ability to concentrate and focus
- Ability to analyze and find weaknesses in opponents' styles
- Ability to think and make decisions quickly in a crisis
- Development of leadership skills and the ability to teach others

Martial arts is one of the few activities that can have so many benefits to its practitioners. **As an instructor, you must never lose sight of the fact that you are the one who is giving these benefits to your students.** This is your real "job description" — helping your students to realize all of these benefits. It is a sacred and incredible responsibility, but one with great rewards as well. There's nothing quite like the knowledge that you've helped someone get over her fear or achieve her dreams.

Remember, it is your job to be an EXAMPLE of these benefits. That way the benefits will become tangible for your students.

Leading by Example

Your students are looking to become like you (at least as far as martial arts go). They want to someday earn your belt and earn your skill and also earn your peace of mind, confidence, and all the other benefits you've received through training.

It is absolutely critical that you keep up your own training. Although you may be busy, you need to at least get the minimum training in. The more you train, the more energy you will have, and the more you'll be able to relate to and help your students. Remember, people will pick up on subtle clues. It is hard for people to believe an out of shape person telling them how training will get them in the best shape of their lives. You can't talk about how important patience is, and then lose your temper all the time. If you're not training, people will wonder *"If training is so great, why aren't you doing it?"*

A person who says one thing and does another is called a **hypocrite**. You should avoid this at all costs, as this will make your students lose trust in you and stop taking what you say to heart. When this happens, you've lost your ability to teach them anything.

By the same token, if you lead by positive example, your students will say *"hey, this stuff really works!"* or *"this guy knows what he's talking about!"* It will now be **easier** to teach your students, because they will listen to you more carefully.

Enthusiasm – Sometimes it is difficult to be excited about your classes. This especially happens if you are teaching 5 or 6 classes every day, and you feel like you are running out of new ideas, or that the students are not progressing.

Here are some tips to keep your energy level high:

- Review the benefits of martial arts. What you are doing is incredibly important.
- Go to www.wikidrills.com to come up with some new ideas.
- Teach every class like it's the most important class you will ever teach. Imagine that you had limited vision into the future, and you knew that one of your students will be assaulted in the next month or one will go to the Olympics in 10 years. How would you teach the class differently?
- Imagine that your class is a trial class. Imagine that there is one student who is planning on quitting after class is over, unless your class is good enough to change his mind.
- Treat a class of 1 or 2 students with the same excitement as a class of 30. Otherwise, you will never have a class of 30 students.
- Periodically ask parents what their child is doing at home that makes them proud. Oftentimes they will credit a good behavior to martial arts.

Authority Vs Influence

This is a very important concept for instructors to understand. Authority is making a decision for someone to do something and having them do it, while influence is making a suggestion to someone and having them make the decision to do it. For instance, if you say *"Give me 10 pushups,"* that's using your authority. However, if you say *"I think you will get better if you practice at home,"* then you are using your influence.

You have authority over the students in the class just because you are their teacher. They'll do the bare minimum of what you tell them in class, just because they "have to", or because you can punish them if they don't. However, you should try to also gain influence over them. Influence can also extend to other areas of their lives, such as influencing them to eat healthier or get more sleep.

How do you get influence? First of all, you have to lead by example. The students must want to be like you, at least in some area of life. Secondly, they have to trust you. Otherwise, when you ask them to do things that they don't see the benefit of it, they won't do it. They have to trust that following you will give them the benefits that you have. They have to believe that you can help them to achieve their goals. Gaining influence is not an easy thing, and it often takes time. However, with good honest work and a positive attitude, you will gain it in the end.

Also, it is very important to notice that authority and influence can be used for good or bad. You have the authority to order students to do drills that are dangerous to them and can lead to injury. It is up to the instructor not to do this. If you did, not only would the students become injured, but you would lose your influence because people would no longer trust that you have the ability to make them better.

Lesson 3: Ten Influential Martial Artists

The martial arts that we practice today have been influenced by literally millions of people down through the ages. The following is a list of eleven people (ten martial artists and one philosopher) who have been some of the most influential. Of course, any list such as this is subject to debate, and the figures below have each been the subject of many entire books. However, knowing a little bit about each and their contributions will help students to understand the current state of our training. As an instructor, it is important to know how our training became like it is today and also to have role models. When you feel adversity in your life, it is helpful to see what other people have been able to overcome. Many of the following people would be excellent role models for current martial arts teachers.

Confucius (~550 BC) – Confucius was not a martial artist, but his teachings did much to influence Asian society and thought. His main teachings were about the **Five Relationships** - between father and son, husband and wife, prince and subject, elder and youngster, and friends. Each person in a relationship has a duty to the other. This shows in the relationships that we have in our martial arts schools.

Bodhidharma (~500 AD) – Bodhidharma was an Indian monk who migrated to China in the 6th century AD. There are a lot of myths and legends surrounding him, and the truth is hard to ascertain. However, the legend is that the monks of the time were physically unable to deal with the strict meditation regimen that Buddhism requires. He purportedly stared at a wall for nine years without speaking. Seven years into his nine, he fell asleep. After this he cut off his own eyelids so it would not happen again. Finally, he understood how martial arts practice could help.

According to Jeffrey Broughton's *The Bodhidharma Anthology: The Earliest Records of Zen*, there is another legend about a time when Bodhidharma spoke with the emperor.

The emperor asked Bodhidharma, *"What is the highest meaning of noble truth?"*

Bodhidharma answered, *"There is no noble truth."*

The emperor then asked Bodhidharma, *"Who is standing before me?"*

Bodhidharma answered, *"I don't know."*

The emperor then asked Bodhidharma, *"How much karmic merit have I earned by ordaining Buddhist monks, building monasteries, having sutras copied, and commissioning Buddha images?"*

Bodhidharma answered, *"None."*

Regardless of the truth of these legends, the important point is that the beginning of the martial arts as we know it can be traced to the moment when someone decided to combine a higher spiritual purpose with fighting. People have fought since the beginning of history, but having the martial arts be more than just fighting is something that originally happened when people decided to add other elements to basic technique.

Miyamoto Mushashi (1584-1645) – Miyamoto Mushashi is a famous swordsman from Japan's feudal era. He is most famous for his book *"A Book of Five Rings,"* called in Japanese *Go Rin No Sho*. He was orphaned at age 7 and when he was only 13, he was challenged by an accomplished samurai. The samurai was armed with a sword and Mushashi only had a stick. Mushashi won the duel, and from that point on, he lived by wandering around the land challenging whoever he could find and seeking enlightenment by way of the sword. He fought in more than 60 duels and six wars, and ended up dying of old age in a cave.

His skill with the blade was so great that he often would only bring a *bokken* (wooden practice sword) to a duel when his opponents would bring swords and spears.

Mushashi was a strange character. After being attacked in a bathhouse and having to fight his way out, he never took another bath for the last few decades of his life. He traveled around in tattered rags and had oily, unkempt hair. Yet, his poetry and calligraphy are some of the most valued of any Japanese artist.

He is considered by many to be the greatest swordsman who ever lived.

Jigoro Kano (1860 -1938) – Jigoro Kano was born into a tumultuous time as Japan was just becoming open to the west after the Meiji Restoration. Jigoro wanted to study martial arts all his life, which is not surprising considering that in his teens he was a 5 foot 2 inch, 90 pound weakling who was beaten up by bullies all the time. However, he didn't start training until he was almost 18 years old.

Kano was very open to different ideas about martial arts and education in general. He took ideas from other styles, western wrestling and boxing, and science and physics. He changed the jujitsu of the day by making it less dangerous. That way, his students could practice on a fully resisting partner instead of just practicing forms. At age 22, only 4 years after he started training, he founded the Kodokan school and the martial art of Judo. The school is one of the oldest surviving martial arts schools, about to celebrate its 125th birthday. Branches have sprung up all over the world. Other innovations that Kano had at the Kodokan were the use of a colored belt system to denote different classes of trainees and the systemization and teaching of the falling technique to beginning students.

Kano was a very busy man. By the time he was 25, he had not only graduated college, but was already a professor and the headmaster of two different universities, in addition to the Kodokan. He was also the first Japanese member of the International Olympic Committee.

Masahiko Kimura (1917-1993) – Kimura was one of Kodokan Judo's most famous students. He helped to popularize Judo by spreading it around the world in a series of famous matches in the mid 20th Century.

Judo of the period was different from most martial arts today, in that advancement in rank was determined only by beating people higher ranked than you, rather than minimum age or time. Thus, Kimura became the youngest ever 5th Dan at age 18. That same year, he lost four matches. Those would be the only four matches that he ever lost in his life. Later on, he would go on to hunt down all of the people who had bested him and defeat all of them.

His dominance was so strong that he would do things like have a strenuous 3 hour sparring session before showing up at the national championship to soundly defeat all his opponents.

Kimura was a bear of a man who did hundreds of pushups daily and simply overpowered many of his opponents. One of his most famous matches was against Helio Gracie. In this match, Kimura manhandled the much smaller Gracie. At one point, Kimura had his legs on Gracie's chest and caused Gracie to go unconscious. Later on, when Kimura shifted, Gracie revived and continued the match! The match ended when Kimura went to lock Gracie's shoulder. Gracie refused to tap, so his corner threw in the towel.

The match ended with mutual respect from both sides. In honor of Kimura's fight, Gracie named the lock that defeated him the Kimura lock in Gracie jujitsu.

Helio Gracie (1913- 2009) – Helio Gracie was a Brazilian man who was sickly as a child. He tried to learn jujitsu, but found that many of the techniques were not suited to his small frame. Thus, he modified the techniques to require an even smaller amount of leverage. He also made good use of the guard position, which was used in Judo but only sparingly. He recognized the value that the guard can have for a smaller person.

Although Gracie's fight career was nowhere near as prolific as that of his sons, he did have his share of marathon matches. He fought one match for fourteen ten minute rounds before it was stopped by police. He also holds the record for the longest match, one that he fought against his former student and lost by knockout from a kick to the head after an amazing 3 hours and 40 minutes!

Choi Hong Hi (1918-2002) – General Choi was another person who was sick as a child. He grew up during the Japanese occupation of Korea and thus learned Japanese Karate techniques. One time, the Japanese put him in jail for a nationalist Korean disturbance, and he taught Karate to the inmates and guards.

General Choi was in the Korean army and rose to the rank of Major-General. He also served as the country's ambassador to Malaysia. General Choi was the person who first suggested the name of Taekwondo when the art was being brought together in the 1950s and 1960s. He served as the head of the International Taekwondo Federation (ITF) for many years, eventually moving to Canada.

Bruce Lee (1940-1973) – Bruce Lee is one of the best known martial artists. His influence is important in a number of ways that might not be known to everyone. First of all, he was a movie star who made several classic films. This helped to popularize martial arts in many other parts of the world besides Asia. It also showed studios that martial arts movies could be profitable. For instance, *Enter the Dragon* cost less than $1 million and made over $90 million! This helped pave the way for other martial arts movies and movie stars, which in turn led to many more people starting to train.

Another way that Lee was influential was his emphasis on physical conditioning. He was able to do one handed pushups on two fingers and was very strong and powerful for his size. He also was the inventor of the style of Jeet Kun Do, and emphasized free flowing arts over classical, more structured arts. In this way he was a forerunner of the MMA revolution that happened after his death.

Jhoon Rhee (1932- Present) – In the second half of the 20th century, many Korean masters went all around the world to spread Taekwondo. One of the most influential in the US was Jhoon Rhee. Rhee has taught many people, including over 300 US Congressmen. He was also one of the first people to ever set a form to music.

Rhee was instrumental in systematizing the business of school operation. Many masters before this time had no grasp of business or organization building, and as a result classes were small and schools often closed. Perhaps his greatest achievement was the invention of the RheeMax foam sparring gear, which allowed people all over the world to train harder with reduced injuries.

Ernie Reyes, Sr. (1947- Present) – Ernie Reyes is a great martial arts master from California. His *West Coast Action Team* was instrumental in pushing the boundaries of creative martial arts and demonstration techniques. This demo team is also quite possibly the most impressive demo team in the world. Reyes and his children also starred in several Hollywood movies.

Reyes is also very active in organization building. He is a fantastic motivator and dynamic performer and speaker. He is also the creator of the Little Dragons curriculum, a method for teaching martial arts to preschool age children.

Lopez Family (Present Time) – The Lopez family is known as the "First Family of Taekwondo," not only in the US but in the world. They have dominated Sport Taekwondo like no other family. In 2005 when all three won the world championship, the USOC stated that never in the history of the US has one family dominated any sport in such a manner. Jean Lopez is the oldest brother, and he is their coach. He also won a silver medal in the world championships. Steven is quite possibly the best Taekwondo player ever. He has lost only one match since 1999, including in his streak 2 Olympic gold medals and 3 world championships gold medals. Mark was the youngest man from any country to win a medal in the world championships— he has one each of gold, silver, and bronze. Sister Diana was not to be outdone, and took her own gold medal in the world championship. In the 2008 Olympics, all three siblings won medals.

Looking at this list, several things are striking. One is how many famous martial artists were small, sick, and picked on as children. Certainly, these early experiences helped to mold them into fierce fighters. Another thing to notice about the list is the lack of diversity. Long ago, martial arts training was reserved for nobles and their sons or the elite in the military. Through the work of many on this list, the number of people training has increased incredibly. First poorer males were allowed to train, then women, then children, etc. Now, we have recognized the positive impact martial arts can have on all people. At many schools there is special training for very young children, older men and women, the disabled, mentally and physically handicapped people, etc. One hundred years from now, we are likely to see many of these people on a new list.

Lesson 4: Communication Skills

The point of communication is to get your message across effectively and without confusion. When there is a breakdown in communication, people will think that you meant something different than what you actually meant. This can cause confusion, difficulty convincing people of your point of view, and lost opportunities. Here are some tips for better communication:

- **Know the nature of communication** – Communication is a "whole body" process, where everything matters. Studies disagree on the exact percentage, but most of communication is non-verbal. This means that things like your tone of voice, posture, eye contact, etc., give much more of the message than your words. Often, this is even subconscious, and you or the other person might not even realize it.

- **Know what you're talking about** – The more you understand what you're saying, the better you will be able to speak about it with other people. If it's something like a debate, get your facts straight beforehand. If you're confused yourself, you're not likely to convince anyone of an opposing viewpoint.

- **Understand Context** – Context means the environment that the communication occurs in. This includes the feelings of the other person. For instance, you might get a very different reaction from someone right after they nailed a great black belt test than right after they lost a tournament.

- **Make Eye Contact** – In some cultures this is disrespectful, but in America it's good to look someone firmly in the eye. This way, you can also sense their body language much more correctly.

- **Use Gestures** – Hand gestures can emphasize your point, but in martial arts class, often you'll be talking about something technical. Bring up another instructor or student and demonstrate together if necessary.

- **Exaggerate** – Don't be afraid to exaggerate to make your point. For instance, if talking about stepping too far backwards, step really far so that everyone can see how you will now not be able to counter. Students can sometimes pick up on this more easily.

- **Relax** – People look up to you and know you're an expert. They want to hear what you have to say. Just be yourself and tell them.

- **Use Personal Stories** – When making a point, talk about how something similar happened in your life. Be careful not to teach an unintended consequence. For instance, when talking about the value of repetition for ingraining a skill, you might mention that you've practiced your falling technique so many times, even though you get drunk and fall down every Friday night you never hit your head. You'd also be teaching the students it's okay to get so drunk you fall down every Friday night.

Lesson 5: Learning Styles

Everyone learns in a different way. **By appealing to many different types of learners in the same class, we can ensure the best delivery of our message to the student.** There is some disagreement within the scientific community over whether or not learning styles have any physiological basis, and on whether teaching to different learning styles actually produces better results. However, this idea is relatively new, and just because something is unproven doesn't mean it's not right.

We all know anecdotal evidence of people who prefer to learn things one way or another. One student might do great at remembering a form but not have a clue when it comes to Korean Terminology. However, for the average student, we don't need to psychoanalyze them and try to change the lesson plan to suit them. We just make sure that our lesson plans can appeal to all types of learners. There should be enough overlap so that all students will be able to understand the material.

When it comes to learning styles, it is also important to recognize that people don't just learn in one style. They may have one strongest, or preferred way to learn, but they will still learn material in the other ways, albeit with much more difficulty.

- **Visual (Spatial) Learners** – Visual learners prefer to see new information and to use images, pictures, or maps to communicate their understanding. They are very good in special tasks and seem to have a great sense of direction. Visual learners like using maps and other representations of complex data. A DVD-ROM and its videos would be fantastic for visual learners.

- **Aural (Auditory) Learners** – Aural learners use sound or music to learn things. They are often great with musical instruments, rhythm, or dancing. They also are good when listening to instructions. These learners can learn Korean Terminology by listening to the mp3 files on a requirements DVD-ROM. The easiest thing for them to memorize is the words to a song.

- **Verbal (Linguistic) Learners** – Verbal learners love words, both spoken and written. They may be very good at reading and writing and may often 'catch' you on things you say that are ungrammatical or have a hidden meaning. These kinds of learners will really appreciate something like "*The Simpsons*." For them, a school handbook provides a wealth of information.

- **Physical (Kinesthetic) Learners** – Physical learners do great in Taekwondo. Not only do they learn things by doing (the main way we teach in class) they also are more comfortable exercising. They often think best while mowing the lawn, taking a jog, or walking down the beach. No one can become successful in Taekwondo without being at least a little bit of a physical learner. You can study the mechanics of board breaking all you like, but you won't know what it's like until you actually break the first board.

- **Logical (Mathematical) Learners** – Logical learners like things to be ordered by patterns that might not be apparent to others. They utilize to-do lists, love science and brain teasers, and like to go through things in a step by step approach. Logical learners are good at doing calculations in their heads. We support these learners by quantifying techniques, for instance with the school records and the scientific training basis of the school.

In addition to the learning styles described above, there are two more that deal with the group dynamics of how people learn.

- **Social (Interpersonal) Learners** – Social learners love learning in a group, especially during class time. They feed off the energy of other people in the class, and like working together to figure things out.

- **Solitary (Intrapersonal) Learners** – Solitary learners may spend a lot of time training on their own. They may learn the basics during class time, but really work on 'perfecting' the technique or 'getting it' at home. They may find the class to 'overwhelming' and prefer to really work through the technique by themselves in their rooms or in a park.

Lesson 6: Personality Types

The study of differing personality types can be helpful in understanding and working with different people. As instructors, we must deal with people who are similar to us and different from us in a variety of ways. There are several systems that have been developed to try to classify people's personality types. The most famous is the MBTI Test, or the Myers-Briggs Type Indicator, first published in 1962. This test is used in pre-marriage relationship counseling, hiring decisions, and career development offices.

Four Dichotomies

The MBTI Test consists of a series of questions to determine which of the following qualities you are closest to:

Extraverted Vs Introverted
Sensing Vs iNtuition
Thinking Vs Feeling
Judging Vs Perceiving

Let's look at each quality in a bit more detail.

Extraverted – Extraverts prefer action outside of themselves. They may be very friendly, talkative people. They draw energy from focusing on people and things.

Introverted – Introverts prefer action inside of themselves. They prefer to think first, focusing more on concepts and ideas rather than people and things.

Sensing – Sensing dominant people prefer concrete data, what they can learn from their five senses. They like proof, and distrust hunches.

Intuition (N) – Intuitive people are more likely to follow a hunch. They don't need to know exactly why something is true to act as if it is. They are also more likely to develop a vision for the future.

Thinking – Thinkers tend to approach things from a rational, more abstract standpoint.

Feeling – Feeling dominant people tend to approach things from a more empathetic standpoint. For instance, when confronted with a homeless person, a thinker might not give money because he knows it will create more beggars, while a feeler might give money because he feels sorry for the beggar.

Judging – Judgers prefer to have things decided and settled.

Perceiving – Perceivers prefer to have things left open ended.

There will be 16 different final results based on this classification. It is important to note that no one will be completely to one side, but it is just what you prefer. Also, thinkers are not 'smarter' than feelers. The test measures only preference, not ability. There is no 'best' type, although some types may be better suited for some professions, or some types may work better with other types.

Isabel Myers created the following table of approximate personality types

ISTJ - Inspector - 11.6%
ISFJ- Protector - 13.8%
INFJ – Counselor- 1.5%
INTJ – Mastermind -2.1%
ISTP – Crafter - 5.4%
ISFP – Composer - 8.8%
INFP – Healer - 4.3%
INTP – Architect - 3.3%
ESTP – Promoter - 4.3%
ESFP- Performer - 8.5%
ENFP- Champion - 8.1%
ENTP- Inventor - 3.2%
ESTJ – Supervisor - 8.7%
ESFJ – Provider- 12.3%
ENFJ- Teacher- 2.4%
ENTJ- Field Marshal 1.8%

Although the ENTJ (also called General or Superleader) is only about 1.8% of the population, many school owners are of this type.

To see what type you are and to learn more, visit the official Myers-Briggs Foundation website at: **http://www.myersbriggs.org/**

Lesson 7: Teaching Techniques

Always remember that **we teach people first and martial arts second.** Here are some generally used techniques to help you to work with your students.

Neuro-linguistic programming (NLP) is a branch of psychotherapy founded in the 1970s. One of the key components of this psychology is the concept of a *Frame*, that is, the context (both inside and outside their heads) through which people perceive events happening around them. People's frames are influenced by past events, their mood, anxieties, fears, etc. For instance, someone who just met a beautiful girl who says "*I'll call you tomorrow*" would react much differently to the phone ringing than someone who is behind on the mortgage and afraid of foreclosure.

Anthony Robbins and Dave Kovar have been instrumental in applying the key NLP concept of framing to teaching martial arts. Often, the problem you may have is that someone insists on looking at things from the 'wrong' point of view. How can you use pre-framing and re-framing to help get your point across?

Pre-framing – Pre-framing is getting someone to see something from your point of view before they have formed their own opinion on the matter. It is useful to get everyone in a positive mindset before a particular event or drill. Pre-framing also includes 'hyping up' upcoming events. Here are some examples of preframing statements:

- "I've got a great class planned for you guys today…"
- "We're just getting started. If you think this is hard, wait for set 2!"
- "This next drill is going to make your back kicks really fast and efficient."
- "I don't expect you guys to be able to do this, but let's see if anyone can prove me wrong."
- "You only have 10 chances to do the best roundhouse kick of your life."

Be careful when pre-framing that you don't hype something up and then not live up to your promise. Sure, what you think is a great class will differ from what each individual in the class thinks, but you can't promise them a great class and then do the same thing you did the last 5 classes. Also, be careful of hyping up individuals, for instance *"I can't wait to see you at the next tournament/test."* Statements like that can be useful, but if they fail, then they might feel like they are letting you down too, or might feel like you weren't really watching/didn't really know their level, if for instance they went to a tournament and got soundly beaten by everyone in their division.

Re-Framing – Reframing is getting someone to view something in a different way after they have already formed an opinion. Often, this involves highlighting a different point of view that they might not have thought of. Sometimes, they might have just formed their opinion out of ignorance.

For instance, someone might say, *"Training in Taekwondo will make my kid a bully."* You might say, *"Actually, the opposite is true. Bullies are usually insecure children, and our students are very confident. Also, bullies often want to 'test' themselves. Our students know that they can test themselves against people who actually know what they are doing."*

Re-Framing is often very important because in your martial arts career you will have to deal with many people with whom you do not agree. You have to be able to make the most of the situation, because it may save students. Remember, if your students quit, there is no way that you can continue to help them.

Should you demonstrate an entire skill or break it down?

This depends on the length of the skill and the ability of the people. For instance, for review of previous belt requirements, it makes sense to show the whole skill. For new skills, especially complex ones, it makes sense to break it down. It also depends on the level and age of the students. Younger students need smaller chunks, maybe only a few moves of a form at a time.

Even if you don't break it down in your demonstration, students should know how it's broken down so that they can work on each move by themselves. Even within each move, you should know how each is broken down to have a better mechanical understanding. Go to the anatomical moves section to fully understand each technique.

When teaching new skills to students, emphasize similarities to the skills that they already know.

Teach students to self-monitor. I.e., teach them what each technique should look like, so that they are able to use the mirror, video tape, or feel, to help correct themselves.

Praise-Correct-Praise or "Criticism Sandwich"

The PCP method works by sandwiching a constructive criticism between specific praises. As instructors, we correct our students because we want them to get better. If we really didn't care about the students, we would just let them keep doing things wrong. It's certainly much easier than trying to change them. However, since we do care about the students, we have to correct them. The problem is that sometimes, if a student only receives criticism, they will become defensive and begin to tune you out. They may also get the feeling that you don't like them. These are both bad outcomes, because it will cause you to lose influence over the student, and you will lose your ability to make them better.

The PCP method attempts to get around this by using praise to help. One example might be:

"Your double kicks are improving quite a bit. Remember to turn your hips fully so that you kick with the top of your foot. There you go, that's much better."

While this method might be useful for some instructors, it can come across as a bit contrived sometimes. As long as you make sure that each student receives praise often enough and also that your criticism is healthy, you don't need to stick to a hard and fast rule.

Notes on Praise and Criticism

Praise – For younger students (especially preschoolers) praise and constant feedback is very important. It doesn't matter if their technique isn't perfect, tell them good job anyway! They are trying really hard, and that will make them try harder. However, for older students and higher ones, be careful of giving false praise. If you tell someone "good form" and it's one of the worst forms that they've done, they will know that you are just being nice or not really paying attention. In either case, your compliments will lose value to them. There are some instructors out there who rarely give compliments. This can get the students frustrated, but they truly treasure the times when they do get a genuine compliment, because they know that they've achieved something out of the ordinary.

Remember, true self esteem doesn't come from someone telling you 'good job' when you know it wasn't. True self-esteem comes from overcoming challenges. Praise should be as specific as possible. Also, when praise is paired with outside feedback, it reinforces your influence in the person's mind. For instance *"You really timed that guy well on your back kick"* makes perfect sense to someone who just scored a point with his back kick in a tournament. Also, praise doesn't have to be explicit. For instance, *"Do you hear how much louder the pad is now that you're turning your hips?"* doesn't give explicit praise, but the person knows that he is doing better due to a specific correction you made.

Be careful of only generic praise, especially when what you're saying could be said by anyone in the dojang, including the grandma watching class for the first time. If all you say is *"good kick"* whenever anyone kicks the paddle really hard, anyone can see that. Tell them what about it made it good or what they can do to make it better. This is not to say that you should never give generic praise, but it should be rare compared to your specific praise. They're coming to train with you because you can tell them things about their techniques that the other people in the room can't. So tell them.

Finally, it is important to remember that you can praise effort or progress if you can't praise results. If someone is working hard, let them know that you noticed and also tell them how confident you are that they will make it to their goal.

Criticism – It is even more important for criticism to be specific than praise. With criticism, you're trying to get them to change something about the way they're doing it. It's true, sometimes you can get someone to kick harder by simply saying *"kick harder."* In that case, it's usually that their body can kick harder and their mind knows how to do it, but for some reason or another they're not. However, if someone is already going to the extent of their skill level, telling them *"kick harder"* without telling them how won't make a difference. You need to tell them to turn their hips over or have a wider stance or keep their leg straight at the moment of impact.

One of the most frustrating things for a student is having an instructor give them unhelpful criticism. They're probably frustrated already because they can't do the technique properly, so you're just going to make them more frustrated. Of course, while they're frustrated, they're going to be even less likely to get it right, which will lead to more frustration. Avoid this by giving them specific instructions, and going through things in a slow and basic way. Have them concentrate on technique only and take out power and speed. Also, you should be a calming influence so that they can relax and get better.

Persuading Through Questions

Persuading through questions is a way to get the students to find information themselves, rather than just telling it to them. This way, it will be easier for them to remember, and you will be certain that they understand you. This will work for technical information as well as behavioral information. For example, you might say *"You know that Bob has a great back kick. Do you think it's a good idea to attack on the open side?"* Or again *"What do you think would happen if you did a front kick with your toes?"* For behavioral persuasion, you could say something like *"Do you think I'm going to be happy to hear if you're failing school?"* You can even ask them questions where they have to make tough decisions that if you made them, they might think they're unfair. For instance *"Do you think it's right if I let you keep your red belt but you don't know your forms?"*

Getting and Keeping Attention in Class

It's very important that the students are focusing on you, the teacher, during class time. This usually isn't so much of a problem if the whole class is doing the same thing. However, it becomes more of a problem when one person or group is performing and the rest is sitting and watching.

The classic way to get attention is to call "Charyut!" which will force everyone to snap to attention stance. However, it might not work so well if everyone was sitting down. Another way is to say *"I need to see everyone's eyes up here."* Or *"Clap once if you can hear me."* It is also important to call out specific individuals who are not focusing, and not let them get away with disrupting the class.

Learning Progression: Set your students up for success.

Learning in martial arts follows macro and micro progressions which are usually, but not always, well defined. There are several benefits of teaching in this way:

- **Safety** – The danger of a move often depends on the skill of the one doing it. Dive rolls are much more dangerous for people who have not mastered regular rolls. You minimize risk when students only try moves they are ready for.
- **Efficiency** – Students learn more quickly, and you are able to easily identify and correct their errors.
- **Sense of Progress** – Students will know that they are moving in the right direction.
- **Sense of Future Progress**- The students will know where they will be in 1 year, 2 years, etc. from now. They will also know that there is much more for them to learn.

Forms are already broken down into moves. Teach a few moves at a time, and then once the students have gotten those, teach a few more. What if the students can't get the first few moves? Break those down as well, into the stances, chambers, and techniques. Repeat over and over until the student is ready to go to the next level. Here is another example of a progression for learning falling.

- Lay down and slap the ground with proper form
- Falling technique from sitting on a soft mat
- Stand, then sit, then falling technique on a soft mat
- Stand, then while sitting, do the technique at different heights
- Standing falling technique on the soft mat
- Jumping falling technique on the soft mat
- Throw with control from a low height on soft mat
- Throw with control from higher and higher on the soft mat
- Repeat the same on the regular mat

Of course, you're going to have students skip some steps. The key is that you don't just show falling technique and then throw someone over your shoulder. Kick low before you kick high. Do single kicks before you do double kicks. Certainly, sometimes you'll want to work on something in a class and one or two students are not at that level. Either let them work on the basics, use your judgment and let them try something, as long as they won't have a higher risk of injury from it. Students usually won't feel the same frustration if they are having trouble picking up something a little advanced as if they were studying their own material.

Macro progressions include something like the belt system, the transition from beginner's class to intermediate to advanced, the transition from student to instructor trainee to instructor to school owner, the transition from learning techniques to sparring drills to sparring, etc. The more progressions are set up, adhered to, and clearly defined, the more success you will have when teaching.

Lesson 8: General Training Effects

The human body is amazing in so many different ways. One is its ability to adapt to almost any situation. This leads to simple strategies for training. How do you stop yourself from getting tired? Train until you are tired many times. How do you not get dizzy? Spin around until you are dizzy. Over time, your body will adapt to whatever stresses you put on it. This is well illustrated in the classic scene from the movie *The Princess Bride* where Vizzini has chosen to battle the Man in Black in a game of wits about which cup he has put poison in.

In the battle of wits between these two characters, Vizzini engages in a long and complicated tirade about how he can use his superior intellect , knowledge of human nature, and psychological analysis of the Man in Black to conclusively determine which cup has been poisoned. At the height, he points to something off in the distance and then switches the cups when the Man in Black looks. He suggests that they drink, and when the Man in Black raises his cup first, Vizzini drinks his.

Vizinni starts laughing about how he has won the battle of wits, and then falls over dead. When Princess Buttercup remarks about the how the Man in Black had put the poison in his own cup, he famously replies:

They were both poisoned. I spent the last few years building up an immunity to iocane powder.

Of course, it goes both ways. If you 'practice' sitting on the couch all day, your body will become suited for that as well. This can be dangerous for instructors who aren't up on their regular training regimen, if you suddenly try to overexert yourself. The effects of this are compounded if you don't take your warmup as seriously as you should.

You will not gain or lose all attributes at once. For instance, when not training, many instructors may lose endurance first, timing second, and strength third. They will generally not lose strategy, as that is constantly being practiced.

This leads to more danger for instructors who try to demonstrate things in front of the class. They can still kick hard, but get tired more quickly. This can combine with not stretching properly to lead to bigger injuries, since they still have good force behind their kicks.

When the shock to the body is too great, injury or death will occur. The iocane powder is a fictional substance, so there is no way to verify the above scene. However, the dosage that the Man in Black took would have had to be precise, and below the toxic level. Also, not every poison can have an immunity built up to it, our body is biologically incapable of defending against everything, especially non-biological chemicals.

This process is similar to what happens in bacteria to make them immune to antibiotics, except that there, individual bacteria die or live based on genetic mutations, and then they reproduce to change the properties of the whole population.

Lesson 9: The Ideal Class

Elements of An Ideal Class

Key- Being good at martial arts requires repetition, but repetition can create boredom. Thus, the little things must be varied. Change counts, targets, directions, competitions, etc.

The following elements can be part of a class. However, most classes will use only some of these elements.

Greeting- Tell a joke, break the ice, get students to put aside outside worries and get mentally ready for class.

Bow-in- Officially start the class.

"Pre-warmup" – Do low range of motion activities (jogging, jumping jacks, etc.) to get students sweating and loosen joints and tendons for better stretching.

Stretching – Do a light stretch to avoid injury. Focus on major muscle groups that you will be using in class.

Conditioning – This is the meat of class. This element can be mixed with or used after the skill element. This includes kicking, sparring, cardio drills.

Skills Work – Review old skills and introduce new ones. Forms, kicks, demos, etc. If the skill is too new, it should be done when the student is fresh, but later on students should know how to perform their skills when tired.

Cool Down Time – Now you can do a deep, long stretch for flexibility. Situps, pushups, and lunges can be used here too.

Talk With Students – Talk to the students about techniques, life, tell a story, etc. For higher students, sometimes ask them to talk to you or the class.

Bow out- Officially end the class.

- Note on talking to students during class - If one or two students are doing something wrong, correct individually. If many students are doing a particular thing, stop the class and tell them all or tell before next drill.
- Make your corrections and drill changes quickly to keep students from getting cold muscles.

Limit Down Time- Have the next drill planned before the last one is over. If unsure, use jogging, partner exercises, repeat drill, etc. to think. Set up drills that need time (ladders, obstacle course, etc.) while students are warming up/stretching.

Disguising Repetition

Herein lies the catch-22 of the martial arts training. You need to do something over and over to get good at it, but doing so is boring. Very few of your students will get the years of repetition required, because they will all quit first. What is the answer? Of course, you have to continually present the same material in a slightly different way. Thus, you get the students to learn without being bored. Here are some ways to disguise repetition:

- Add another move. Add in a jump, pushup, etc. before or after the move you are working on. Add in another move to the end of a long combo.
- Vary the kicking leg, front or back, left or right, jumping kick or standing, spinning, etc.
- Vary the targets. Kick the air, wavemaster, BOB, paddles, hogus, etc. Doing a set of kicks in the air and then on a pad feels different.
- Turn the move into a game. Who can do the most kicks or the highest? Use the move in a relay race.

Lesson 10: Student Retention

Student retention is one of the most important things in having a good school. Without retention, you will never have a high number of students. Also, without retention, you will never get the critical high belt helpers to make your life easier. In order to get high retention, you first need to know why students might quit:

Note, that often what matters is not the actual situation, but what the student perceives the situation to be. If you care about a student, but don't show it, they may get the idea that you don't care.

- **"Good Enough Training"** – If you are always just going to the bare minimum and never really trying to improve, the students may leave.

- **Unfair or Disrespectful Treatment of Students/Uneven Application of Discipline** – Don't have a "teachers' pet" because all those students who are not your favorites may leave. It's good to have standard punishments, or tiered ones based on age or belt level. For instance, if all black belts who forget their belt have to do 50 pushups, there isn't a problem. However, if some students have to do it and others don't, then you have a problem.

- **Lack/Perceived Lack of Knowledge of Instructor** – If in the bottom of his heart, the student doesn't think that you can make him better, then he is not likely to stay.

- **Personality Clash** – Sometimes, you will just not get along with certain students, or more likely their parents. You should take steps at first to resolve the differences. Try to ignore things, see things from their perspective, etc. However, if after all this, you still don't get along with them, it's best to let them go. One problem student can cause an incredible amount of damage in your school. This will usually be with the instructor, but it could also be a class of two students or two parents. Try to have them in separate classes, or sit down together to talk about it.

- **Failure to Follow Through on Promises** – If you always say you'll help a student, or if you promise to teach the children discipline, then you have to do that. If you don't, then students will lose trust in you and may quit.

- **No Sense of Progress** – If the student spends time and money in training, but doesn't feel like they are getting better, they are not likely to stay. At first, remind them of the progress vs. time graph (found in the KAT handbook) and let them know that the higher they get, the harder it is to progress. Also, usually in the middle belts, students may get unmotivated. Let them know that this is normal, and now is the time that they will learn to follow through on commitments.

- **Not Seeing the Benefits** – Of course, the benefits of martial arts come over time. However, sometimes, a situation can develop where people believe that the training will not help get them the benefits it should. For example, if the instructor is overly-critical, coming to class might be a source of stress rather than a release. You will lose students this way.

- **Injury/Fear of Injury** – These injuries could be from Taekwondo or from outside activities. Also, if someone thinks that they will get hurt, they will be less likely to do those activities. This usually comes up in relation to sparring. To help them avoid fear of injury, make sure that they are doing drills appropriate to their age/skill level/injury. I.e., don't make someone with bad knees do plyometrics.

- **Burnout** – This often goes along with injury. Students sometimes get so excited, that they train a lot. Sometimes, this causes them to put other areas of their life on hold, and then when they get behind in them, they drop out of TKD. Avoid burnout by limiting the training of younger students. Also, make sure all students balance hard training with fun activities and also periods of rest.

- **No Goals** – If the student does not know where they want to go with their training, they will be less likely to remain excited. Set goals together. The belt system provides perfect feedback and a set of goals.

Keep setting goals even for those students who are already black belts.

- **Change in Policy/Schedule** – Sometimes, you will need to change the curriculum or schedule. Unfortunately, in a large school, there will be a few people who do not like the new way. Also, many people are naturally resistant to change.

- **Class/Student Mismatch** – This is not usually a problem at KAT, because of the large numbers of classes and flexibility of our schedule. However, sometimes someone is in a class that is too easy or too hard for him. He may become either bored or frustrated. Also, this includes having beginning students spar too soon, especially without proper instruction (i.e., have a "Sparring 101" class).

- **Getting Out of the Routine** – This is often the case when students who seemed to love everything about class suddenly stop coming. It's not that the don't want to be there, but once they stop training for a month or so, they feel almost like they're no longer part of the class or that everyone is ahead of them. They're often high belts who have forgotten their form, maybe after an illness, tough semester, or extended vacation. Now, they feel like they'll embarrass themselves and the school if they come back. Encourage them to start slowly.

- **Moving** – Oftentimes, students will move away and be unable to continue training. Always keep them in contact with the school via emails and newsletters. Also, help them to find a school in their new home. Often, they will still refer people from their old home to join the school.

- **Financial Difficulties** – Sometimes, due to a career change or life event, students may no longer be able to afford training.

- **"Not for them."** – I include this last one because it is often a reason why students may take a free trial or a 6 week beginner program but not continue. However, due to the amazing number of benefits of martial arts, this one is usually more a case of you, as the instructor, not getting them to understand all of the benefits that they could achieve. Still, sometimes people are at a point in their lives where they do not choose to engage in healthy behaviors, and often nothing can be done to deter them.

In a nationwide research study conducted by **Gary Gabelhouse** for Fairfield Research, they found that of everyone in America who had trained in Taekwondo at one time, 86% had quit. These are the reasons that they came up with.

Reason Why Quit	% of Quitters
Personal & Job Time Constraints	31%
Moved Away From School	23%
Just Lost Interest	18%
Injury/Medical Problem	13%
Classes Ran Their Term	8%
Finances/Cost of Classes	7%

It is interesting to note that over half (54%) of the people quit for reasons that had nothing to do with the quality of the school. However, if you make the school an inseparable part of the students' lives, they will stay. At KAT, we've had students not move or put off moving out of town just because of the school.

Always assume that you can stop a particular student from quitting. It's not true, but by thinking that way, you will end up stopping many that you thought you could not stop. It always hurts to have your students leave, especially in the beginning. But you have to know that everyone, even great teachers, lose many students. Bruce Lee probably lost hundreds of students in the few years he was teaching. I'm sure Helio Gracie has lost thousands, or even tens of thousands, in the decades that he's been teaching.

On a final note on students quitting, it is important to note that the more proactive you are, the better. If you notice signs that a student is veering off course and correct them immediately, they will be less likely to develop into a full fledged reason to quit. For instance, if you notice that a student is heading for burnout, order him to take a few classes off. If someone has misses several tests and is not quite ready for the next one, offer a free private lesson or two. If you changed the schedule and then noticed some people not coming, sit down with them and plan out a good training regimen. If someone has an injury, explain to them how to still train around it. Doing little things like this ahead of time is the best way to stop people from quitting. The most important thing is to start emailing or contacting students when they start missing classes. It's probably innocuous, but there might be a problem. Sometimes you will have to talk for a while to get to the root of the issue, but usually you will get there and then know what to do to resolve it.

Why Students Stay

Students will stay if the program has good quality and value and they see their own progress. What things contribute to making them want to stay?

Excellent Value – The classes shouldn't be too expensive, and the students should always feel like they're getting more than their money's worth. They should feel like they're 'cheating' us, i.e., getting more out of the training than the money they're putting in.

Challenging Curriculum – The material that you teach and how they advance through the belts is incredibly important. This is usually set by the school, and not the individual instructors. If they need to work hard to succeed, but are not overwhelmed, this is the ideal situation. The curriculum must be easy enough for white belts but not bore the black belts.

Focus on Black Belt – For color belts, having the focus on getting a black belt and knowing that they can achieve it are very important. For black belts, different goals are necessary.

A Sense of Progress – Students who know that they're getting better will not want to leave.

School Community – This is especially important for middle school age children and adults. If the school is where all their friends are, they are not going to leave. The need for a community is a fundamental part of human nature that is mostly unsatisfied in modern life. Students also feel a responsibility to their junior ranks, and a debt of gratitude to their senior ranks.

Motivating Instructor – Sometimes students will keep training because of the instructor and how he or she motivates them. For instance, when one student is having a problem, you could magnify that problem and show how he could overcome it. For example, if the student was tired from a bad night's sleep, you might say something like *"I know that you could not sleep for a week, and still work harder than most of the other students in class!"* This will motivate him and reframe his problem into not being so bad.

Lesson 11: Safety First

Thoughts of safety should permeate everything you do in your class. Most of the lessons in this book, in fact, are devoted to safety, and there are tips in each section to help make your classes safer.

It is important to realize that we can never have perfectly safe classes. It is also important to realize that in martial arts exercise, we trade one type of danger for another. We trade the risk of inactivity for the risk of activity. For instance, when an overweight man sits in the parents section and watches his kid, he is increasing his risk of heart disease. When the same man takes a class with moderate exercise, he is decreasing his risk of heart disease, while increasing his risk of a twisted ankle, bruised shin, etc.

Martial arts training should be a net health benefit. The risks of inactivity should outweigh the risks of activity. We can do nothing about the risks of inactivity, thus we must focus on minimizing the risks of activity. Although a student might be injured slightly in class, his overall health should have improved greatly since starting lessons. The other thing to take into account is the danger of physical attack on the streets. While the risk of this happening is low, the risk to a student's health if it does happen is high if they have not been trained properly.

Recently a parent in our school remarked that his wife was too overprotective, not allowing her son to get a drivers license, although he was past the legal age. I remarked that if parents are too overprotective, then students will not be allowed to learn from small mistakes. It is the same for parents who give their children credit cards from the "Bank of Dad" and treat them as a credit card company would. These children learn valuable lessons with $15-$20 'credit card debt' and pay a few dollars in interest penalties. These same children are much less likely to go out and rack up thousands of dollars in credit card debt when they become adults. It's the same for us in our school. By allowing the students to experience contact in a safe, controlled environment, they can make small mistakes and learn from them. If they are ever attacked on the street, those times getting hit while wearing pads will help them avoid getting hit while not wearing pads.

Perhaps the most important safety tip is to never force students to do what they refuse to do. You must push students beyond their comfort zone and preconceived limits, but you need their permission. Use common sense, and whenever trying out new drills (especially if you make them up yourself), try them out with a limited group and with less speed at first. Here are some more safety tips:

- When an out of shape student first starts class or jumps to a higher class, remind him that he should step to the side if he feels too exhausted to continue. Look for these students and force them to sit out if necessary. Injuries are much more common when a student is too exhausted to perform his technique correctly.
- Keep a log of all injuries in the school and how they happened. Periodically analyze these reports and make changes to teaching as required. Specifically, do not repeat any drill where there was a major injury until you are certain the drill is safe.
- Modify drills for certain students who have factors who make them more likely to get injured. Recommend students with previous injuries or weak spots to wear braces and tape as appropriate.
- Keep first aid kits well stocked and handy in your school at all times.
- Make sure someone is always available to call 911.
- Watch parents as well as children. Older parents and grandparents might be more at risk of needing an ambulance than students in the class.
- Follow the principles of good training area design in the Legal Issues lesson.
- Always make sure students wear appropriate padding for contact.
- Don't allow students who are contagious to practice, and prohibit students with open wounds from grappling or other contact.
- Have a plan for cleaning and disinfecting your school regularly.
- Train seriously. Train with the knowledge that any one of your students could be attacked on the way home, or in 1 week, or in 1 year.

Lesson 12: Warm-ups

Warm-ups are extremely important in martial arts training. It will increase body temperature and blood flow. Most of the functions of warming up can be accomplished passively, by sitting in a sauna or hot tub. These activities should include large body exercises, exercises specific to martial arts, and stretching. Warm-ups will give the following benefits:

- Increasing cardiac output and body temperature. More blood goes to the muscles which helps them to perform.
- Stimulating joint lubricants. This loosens the joints and helps them turn more easily.
- Increasing the rate of energy producing chemical reactions.
- Getting the student in the right frame of mind to begin training. It's important to let them forget about their daily cares and focus on their training.
- Students with injuries should take extra time on warm-up.

You still must disguise repetition during your warm-ups. The key to a really good warm-up is to elevate the body temperature, loosen up the muscles and joints, and get the student mentally prepared for class. Simply put, warming up increases performance. Here are a few warm-up drills that you can use:

In-Place Warm-up: This works particularly well with a large class that you feel would take a long time to warm up. You can do exercises like jumping jacks, windmills, steps, high knees, etc. to get the class warm. It also works well to intertwine the stretches with the warm-up drills.

Circle Jogging: You could choose to start the class with jogging. You can have them just jog, or you can have them carry out exercises on your command. I.e., 1 for pushups, 2 for situps, 3 for toasters, etc. You can also have them do exercises while they're running, such as jumping jacks, high knees, etc.

Circle Drills: Usually after jogging, you can have the students do drills in a circle. For instance, knees up on the long side, jog on the short side, and knees up again on the other long side. You can add in steps, stretching kicks, basics, etc.

Relay Races: Students love to compete over small things. Relay races are a great way. Make sure one line goes twice if it has one less person. You can have them do something then run, then do it again, then run again, or just do something down at the far side. Some good races involve running down and doing their form as fast as they can, rolling techniques, flying side kicks, pushups, situps, etc. Penalize students for cheating. Try to make different things so each line can have a chance to win. I.e., count to 10 in Korean and then run to the other side would help smarter but not faster kids.

Animal Exercises: Animal exercises work great in relays or by themselves. They include: Duck walk, frog jumps (jump long and high) bunny jumps (jump short), bird flying (jump long and flap hands) bear crawl, crab walk (backwards), snake slithers (on your belly), tiger runs (like bear crawl but both hands move together), and shrimping.

Line Drills: Instead of relays just have the students work their drills in their lines. Include stepping, kicking, etc. drills.

Partner Exercises and Stretching: This a good warm-up. See the section on partner exercises for more detail.

Forms: Have the students warm up with their forms. Include some calisthenics in between each form, i.e., 10 pushups.

Paddleball or other Games: Used sparingly, paddleball is a fantastic warm-up.

Self Warm-up: Sometimes for competition classes, having the students warm themselves up is appropriate. Also, you can have everyone be in a circle and suggest one warm-up exercise each.

Shadow sparring: Especially for competition, this can warm up the students and get them in the right frame of mind.

Group Competition Drills: Let each half of the class face each other and say "Let's see who does the highest high-knees" or something of the sort. They'll work harder because it's a competition.

"Circle of Death" Each person goes with each other one and does a certain exchange of techniques.

Weaving Drills: Each person goes and does a kick in front of each other one as they weave through.

Lesson 13: Basics and Traditional Techniques

School Orientation

The school orientation is like the "basics of the basics." This is something that all new students should go through in the first class, or at the very least the first week. Once someone has been through the orientation, they are "officially" a student.

When: The orientation can be done before class, or during class. If during class, try to do it when the class breaks up for skill training, instead of during the warm-up. That way, they won't be so confused by trying to learn a skill like chun-ji before they even know attention stance.

Where: Usually, it's good to bring them by the belts and school rules, right off the mat.

What: Explain to them the following things
- Explain the school rules. Tell them that the rules serve two main purposes. The first is **Safety.** Tell them that following common sense rules will help to prevent the majority of injuries. The second purpose is **Efficiency**. Explain that the reason that we line up in belt order is not because the white belts are unimportant, but rather so that everyone is looking right at someone more experienced than they are. That way, it will make it easier for them to learn. Do not read over every rule; just tell them the most important ones.
- At this point, you can also explain any school banners or slogans, and how now they should see themselves as part of the family. Explain that the other students will be excited to help them, and to ask them questions whenever they are confused.
- You can briefly explain the belt system. They will likely have some questions, so answer them without talking too much. Teach them how to tie their own belts. For younger children, just tie it on them, and tell them that they should practice at home.
- Show them how to bow to the flags when entering and exiting the school. Explain that in Taekwondo, no one just bows to another person, but both people always bow to each other as a sign of mutual respect. Remind them to ask permission to leave the school.

- Teach them attention (*cheryut*) stance and ready (*choombie*) stance. Teach them the relax (*shu*) command and how they cannot move until the command is given. They will often move without realizing it. For younger children, make it a 'statue' game, to see who moves first.
- If there is more time left over, proceed to horse stance and punch or chambering for blocks.

How: Remember, that you may be one of the first martial artists that they've ever talked to! It's important that you come off as professional, patient, and excited. Parents will be watching you carefully as well.

- Teach the students immediately to say *"Yes, sir!"* It needs to be built into habit. Most of the time they'll say that they get it and then you say *"Does everyone understand?"* and they'll say *"Yeah."* **You must reinforce discipline right in the beginning!** Many children who come to your academy have acted up in school and they will be looking to test you and see if they can continue to mess around in the dojang. Other times, the structure and discipline of the arts is just so foreign that they need a while to get used to it.
- Most of the people will be very excited, often looking at the other groups. Remind them to focus their eyes on you, because that is where they will learn. Tell them that no one will get a black belt without patience and discipline. However, tell them that they *can* get a black belt, if they want it enough. Many instructors always saw themselves as black belts, but many students who come in can not even imagine it. Many actually think that they will never make it to green or even yellow. You need to make them see it as a real possibility for them.
- Do not try and teach too much right away. For you, the things contained in the orientation are so basic, you probably don't even think of them. For instance, you wouldn't think of teaching someone how to eat by saying, "lift your fork, now open your mouth, now close it, now chew several times, now swallow, etc." You'd just say, "here is a hamburger, just eat it." You have to put yourself in the new student's mindset. What's boring to you is exciting to them. They will be thrilled to go home and practice choombie over and over.
- Be serious about the importance of basics. Tell them that their individual moves and stances are like bricks, and the forms and other

movements are like houses built out of those bricks. If the individual bricks are weak, you'll never make a good house. It will just fall over. If the bricks are strong, then you can make a large building.

Chambering

Chambering is an intermediate movement in the traditional side of TKD to increase power by making a technique longer. Chambering is not used in the sport or practical self defense components of training. Rules of Chambering:

1) Distance is required for power. Thus, chambered techniques should start as far as possible away from where they are intended to finish. For instance, to do a left hand low block, you should chamber upwards and to your right.

2) Both hands must turn together. This also increases power. The only exception is when a hand is just a supporting hand. In that case, it does not turn.

3) Both hands must move together. This is so that both hands will get to their final positions at the same time.

4) Chamber knife techniques with knife hands.

Lesson 14: Paddle Drills

Paddle drills are an important part of a Taekwondo class. Students love them because they provide immediate feedback on how they performed their techniques. They are also great because students get the sense of hitting something. Here are a few important things to remember with regards to paddle drills:

- Make sure students hold paddles correctly. Generally, the laces should be down (for roundhouse kicks).
- Make sure students hold paddles firmly. They should stay in one place and give some resistance to the kicker.
- Paddle drills can help in timing or movement reading if the holder does a good job.
- Paddles should ideally be held close to the body or face, but can be held farther for added safety of the holder, especially for low belts.
- Remember, holding paddles is a skill too. This is also something people need to practice.

Here are some paddle drills that work well:
- Don't forget the basics. Let students just practice one kick over and over in place or going up and down the dojang.
- Let students practice by varying the timing or distance by holding out the pad sharply or by stepping forwards or back.
- To improve strength, use paddle drills with plyometrics or ripcords.
- Work on combinations. A "school combination" could work well for this one.
- Work on steps with drills. Have the students do a kick, recover, move, and then do another kick.
- Paddle sparring is a great training. Have one student hold for any kick and the other student kick for the entire round.
- Use the other paddle as an object to be avoided or hold a foam sword in one hand. After they kick, try to hit them with the sword as they have to try to get away.

- For punches, hold the paddle against the chest to practice taking the impact.

Lesson 15: Partner Drills

Working with a partner can help students, especially beginning ones, to progress in training. Partners can work with each other on an individual level, and it can help build camaraderie in the school. Here are a few things to keep in mind when doing partner drills:

- Pair up people appropriately. While this will usually not be a problem, sometimes certain students are uncomfortable with each other. Avoid size mismatches, unless with experienced students who can do it safely.
- Sometimes for smaller children you should pair them up, as they will spend ages trying to find a partner who is 'exactly' their height or just pick their friends.
- Be sure that students don't use the partner training as an excuse to talk with their friends during class.

Here are some partner drills:

Plyometrics

- Have the partners face each other. One partner puts his hands out at the waist, chest, or shoulder level. The other partner then does knees up (right, left, alternating, or both.)
- Any plyo jumps can be done while facing each other. This helps a lot for encouragement.
- High Fives and High Tens work particularly well.
- Have the partners both face the same direction. One holds one leg and the other does single leg jumps, making sure to launch his knee high up into the air.
- One partner can make the turtle position, while the other does ski jumps back and forth. For less able partners, the partner on the ground can lie down.
- For the leapfrog jumps, one partner can place his hands on his knees and flatten out his back. The other partner jumps either side to side or front to back, placing his hands on the other's back to get more spring. A variation is that the partner can jump over and then turn around and come through the legs.

Control Drills

- With the partners facing each other, have them do crescent kicks over the other partner's outstretched arm. For added difficulty, add a tight circle around the crescent kick.
- Do horse stance and punch while the partners are facing each other. They should not touch each other.
- Call out a body part and have one student do a precise strike to that part.

Conditioning Drills

- Have partners face each other in horse stance. Have them hit shins, forearms, etc. together in a figure 8 pattern. Not recommended for younger children.
- **Partner Pushups** – Have partners face each other and do a pushup. When they come up, they have to give each other a high five.
- **Partner Situps** – Have them lock their legs and come up together. Have them clap hands or knuckles at the top. Also add twists or pad work. Side situps also work well.
- **V Situps** – One partner holds the other's legs on his shoulders, while partner does situps. This works stretching and stomach muscles.
- **Throwing the Legs** – One partner lies down and grabs the other's ankles. The top partner throws the bottom partner's legs down and the bottom partner should try not to let them hit the floor.
- **Scissor Drill** – One partner lies on the ground and while keeping the legs 6 inches off the ground, scissors back and forth. Other partner must jump out and back. For partners with less coordination, have them jump next to their partner.
- **Figure 8 or back and forth** – Have partners go back and forth or make figure 8s with their legs.
- **Counting** – Have one partner count (and encourage) while another does drills, such as jumping over a pad, continuous double kicks, etc.
- **Vs. Drills** – Have them stay back to back and try to push each other, or face to face and hook legs and try to pull each other to the other side of the dojang.
- **Wheelbarrows** – Have the students make a wheelbarrow and race. You can include pushups or one pushup each time to jump forward.

- **Resistance** – Have the students hold the belt from the back or use ripcords to let their partners work on their explosion.

Stretching

- **Front to Front** – Do the double hamstring stretch, butterfly stretch, and open the legs while facing. Pull on your partner's belt to help open their legs. Stretch from side to side and to the front and back.
- **Back to Front (Back)** – Do the same while pushing down on the partner from the back.
- **Wall (Floor) Assisted** – PNF Stretching is particularly helpful here. Make sure to lock the knee and maintain proper positioning. Ax kick, roundhouse, and side kick work well here.

Other Drills:

- One Step Sparring, Paddle Drills, Grappling, Sparring, etc. are all partner drills. Drills for these disciplines are covered in their respective chapters.
- Stances Game – Have the students do a good long or back stance. The partner mirrors them and then tries to off-balance their partner.

Lesson 16: Promotion Tests

The promotion test is the most formal event for a martial arts school. This is a public demonstration of the skills of the students, and often family members, guest masters, and community members are in attendance. It is critical that the test runs smoothly and that students have a positive experience when they are ready to pass to the next level in their training.

Masters and higher ranking black belts will sit at the head table and judge the candidates. The test giver will run the students through their techniques so that the people at the head table can judge them. The objective of the test giver is to let the students shine and put their best on the floor.

- **Be serious and professional** - This is a very important moment in the students' careers. *The test is about them, not you!*
- **Know the requirements well**.
- **Prepare test and combinations ahead of time** – This is especially true for beginning test givers.
- **Start from simple techniques** – If you want to make the students do combinations, build them slowly by adding one technique at a time.
- **Always demonstrate, especially unclear moves** – Confusion in the test group is a bad sign. Make sure they know what you want them to do. Don't show the whole form, just the first couple of moves. Demonstrate on the same side.
- **Put energy in your voice** – Be loud and confident. The students are nervous and looking to you for stability.
- **Use proper commands**- Cheryut, choombie, pahroh, etc.
- **Let the students show what they know** – Don't get in the way, but challenge them.
- **Present techniques they know in a slightly different light** – Use different combinations, forms facing different ways or in different shapes.
- **Use simple, 'easy' techniques.** Techniques like horse stance and punch, chun-ji, simple kicks, etc., can break the ice or bring a nervous group back from a mistake.
- **You can use 'optional' techniques** – This will let more skilled students shine without frustrating less skilled ones.

Lesson 17: One Step Sparring

One step sparring is an important, but often overlooked part of the curriculum. One step sparring used to be more important— in fact, it used to be a major way that people trained before the advent of sparring pads. One Step Sparring is not realistic in the fact that people would attack you with a long stance and punch and furthermore, signal to you that they were about to do so. However, the reason that it is part of the curriculum is that there are several important things that we learn from One Step Sparring that we rarely, if ever, practice in the rest of the curriculum.

- **Body Targeting** - In sparring, targeting is limited to 'body' or 'head' Of course, this is much too simplistic. Students should learn to attack the temple, sternum, groin, and other anatomical weaknesses. Students should work on using the appropriate knuckle or condoyle to target the weak spot.

- **True Combinations** – Students should learn how to combine kicks, blocks, locks, throws, etc. together. Students must learn how a previous action affects their partner's body to proceed to the next one. Some curriculum techniques are only taught in One Step Sparring.

- **Reaction Time** – Students must react quickly and decisively.

- **Body Practice** – Students should work on a real person to practice their targeting and reacting.

- **Tradition** – One Step Sparring is an important traditional practice that links us to the past.

- **Creativity** – If you allow students to make up their own techniques and combinations, they will get excited to make new combinations and they will understand the underlying combinations better as well.

- **Psychology of Hitting** – Most students will have no trouble striking a pad, but would think twice before fully striking another human. This hesitation can be very detrimental in true self defense settings. By striking at, but not striking, another human, they can begin to decondition themselves away from their natural inclination never to hurt another person.

How to teach One Step Sparring:

Teach One Step Sparring as you would teach any other technique. Some specific ideas include putting students in groups (circles, lines, etc.) and having others quickly attack them, so that the students can practice their techniques quickly and without hesitation.

Lesson 18: Teaching Forms

For many schools, the forms (kata, poomsae, patterns, etc.) are the backbone of the curriculum. They are often the most difficult thing for students to learn for their rank exams. How can you teach students their forms so that they can do them beautifully?

Before students learn a form, they should first understand all the techniques that the form contains. This includes stances, hand techniques, kicks, and chambers. Practice these techniques in place or in line drills up and down the floor. Having a good foundation will make the form that much easier to learn.

Once they are good with basics, let them learn a few moves at a time. Let them really focus on perfecting those moves before you let them learn the next set. After they have learned the whole thing, keep them interested with some of the following modifications.

While Learning:
- Practice individual moves in line drills.
- Practice the form with only the footwork and kicks.
- Practice the form while facing different directions.
- Do forms on the instructor's count, so that you can check each move for errors.
- Do 'Tension Forms'. Practice each move as slow and hard as you can. Allow students to kihap with a long, distorted sound.

When Form is Decent:
- **Substitute Moves** – For instance, change every punch into a double punch, switch knife hands and closed fists, etc.
- **Substitute Stances** – Change every long stance into a back stance, etc.
- **Speed Forms** – Do the form as fast as possible. If they can do this, then the form is firmly planted in their mind.
- **Pattern Forms** – Get with a small group and make an artistic pattern by all doing the form together.
- **Round Forms** – Just like singing a round in choir, have one person (line) start, and then after they have done one move, the next, and so on.

- **Meditation Forms** – Have them do the entire form in their head, visualizing perfect technique. If you touch them on their shoulder, they have to stand up and do the move that they were on.
- **Change Directions** – Let them do the form on your count, but at your signal, they have to turn 90 degrees to the left in the middle of the form, and continue from there.
- **Applications** – Have people attack with the reverse of the form from all directions, while the person doing the form applies his techniques.
- **Distraction Forms** – Make a square around the person doing the form. People on the outside can do anything but step into the square. If the person doing the form messes up, he has to do pushups. If not, the people outside must do it. Alternatively, you can have others throw soft pads at the person doing the form so he is not distracted. Be careful with sensitive children when doing this drill.

When the forms are great and you need an extra challenge:

- **Mixed Form 1** – Do the stances from one form with the hand techniques from another. For instance, all the stances from form one with the hand techniques from form two.
- **Mixed Form 2** – Do move one from form one, then move two from form two, then move three from form three. This one is incredibly difficult.
- **Backwards Form** – Have them do the form as if they were videotaped and the tape is being rewound. Having to chamber backward will be extremely confusing.

A very successful game for teaching forms is to have all the students sit down. Let them come up one at a time and then show the form. If they do a move incorrectly, beep them and make them sit down. They earn one point for each move they do correctly, and then one with the most points wins. You can vary what you require, i.e., just a mostly good move, or perfect stances, chambering, etc. You can also award 'lifelines' to let them ask someone else or the instructor to help them get past a difficult part. If they finish, award 'bonuses' for great chambering, stances, or power.

Levels of Knowing

When can you really say that you 'know' your form? In truth, a form can always be practiced more and learned better. You can use the following five levels of knowing a form to help your students understand where they are and what they need to work on next:

Level 1: They understand a little bit about the form and things like what some of the moves are or what pattern the form makes.

Level 2: They now know all of the moves from beginning to end and can execute them all in sequence.

Level 3: They now can do all the details correctly. This means that they have correct chambering, the path of their moves is correct, the stances have the correct weight distribution, etc.

Level 4: They can now do all of the above and add power as well.

Level 5: They can now do the form so well that it takes on an artistic beauty of its own. Someone watching this form can be inspired deep within.

These levels are helpful because many students idea of 'knowing' or 'mastering' a form is far different from their instructor's idea. Explaining this to them can give them more motivation to keep working.

Lesson 19: Teaching Sport Combat (Grappling and Sparring)

Teaching combat (grappling and sparring) is different than teaching other techniques for several reasons. Here are some of the issues that you will have to consider:

- **Individuality** – When teaching standard curriculum techniques (i.e., forms) you want everyone to perform the technique in the same way, without regard to personal preference, body shape/size, etc. When teaching combat, this is exactly the opposite. What works for one person may not work for another. Thus, teaching must be tailored to each individual. This is a tremendous drain on an instructor's time.
- **Injury/Fear of Injury** – Most students are not scared of hurting themselves during a regular class, but the fear of injury goes up sharply once contact and unpredictability are introduced. Also, the injury rates go up as well.
- **Competition Issues** – When students lose, they may feel like they need to drop out, and when they win, they may become too complacent in their training or feel like they already know everything.
- **Other Training Suffers** – If your promotion and competition requirements are different, students may focus so much on competition that they do not advance in belt level, either because they do not work on their requirements, or because they want to win before moving up in divisions.
- **Loss of Students** – If your student is defeated by someone from another school, they may want to switch to that other school. Unscrupulous masters may watch to see which of your competitors are the best, and then invite them to train for free when you are not looking.
- **Over Reliance on Results** – Students may read too much into results of a competition, when in fact competitions are not real fights.

Although there are many negative issues regarding competition, there are many reasons why it is good as well. Combat gives tremendous confidence increases to students, and training for competition gives great motivation for students to work harder. First, when introducing sparring, the most important tip is to work gradually. You shouldn't make people spar before they are ready. A good progression could be as follows:

- **1. Have students first learn techniques (kicks, punches, etc.) in the air or with targets (paddles, bags, etc.)** – This will help them to be comfortable throwing the techniques and not worry about the mechanics during sparring. Also include reaction drills, drills with steps, etc. Simulate an opponent's counter with foam swords, paddles, etc.

- **2. Have students work on choreographed sparring drills with increasing levels of contact with a competent partner** – This will get them used to contact, from both ends of it. This will also get them used to the various techniques that make up sparring. Vary the amount of improvisation allowed. For instance, start with simple techniques like when one attacks with a fast kick, the other slides back and then throws a double kick. Increase to offering each student two or three options.

- **3. Allow Limited Sparring** – This could be situations such as no head contact, light contact, etc. This will help the person get used to the idea of sparring, as well as the various techniques necessary.

- **4. Full Sparring** – Only after the person has experience going through all the steps and confidence gained from it should he be allowed to do full sparring. Of course, much more work at all levels will be required from here on out.

It should be noted that the time for each student to feel comfortable in each phase will be different, and that once they progress to the next phase, they will still benefit from all the previous ones. Olympic champions still kick paddles every day. Here are some specific sparring drills to help your competitors become better:

- **Zero Sum Hogu Drills** – It's hard to over-emphasize how important it is to repeatedly drill each and every movement, attack and counter, etc. with full speed. Make sure both competitors are actively trying to score, and most of the drills should be 'zero sum games.' In game theory this simply means that both players cannot 'win.' This is accomplished by making their objectives contradictory. For instance, one player attempts to kick and the other attempts to move out of the way. For mismatches, adjust other factors to ensure each competitor wins about 50% of the time. In the previous example, the distance between the players when the kick is launched affects the outcome. If the kicker is too fast, increase the distance, if too slow, decrease it. Eventually each pair of competitors will find a distance where it is equally difficult for each to win.

- **Limited Sparring** – Limit the players to force them to improve on one area of their game. For instance, if a player always kicks with his right, make him kick only with his left. The advantage is that it will force each player to improve their deficiencies. Other examples of ways to limit sparring include (only kicks, only punches, only a certain technique, only double kicks, only attacking, only defending, only neutralizing an opponent, only reacting to a partner's motion, only faking and trapping, changing the ring size and shape, hands tied behind the back, etc.) Also, you can limit sparring to one exchange, to help encourage setting up techniques better.

- **Sparring Games** – There are several games to help students learn to spar better.

    o **King of the Ring** – Especially good for point sparring or 'sudden death overtime' two students spar and the winner is the one who scores first. The loser sits down, and the next student comes forward to challenge the winner. He must make it through all students to be the 'King of the Ring.'
    o **Flag Sparring** – To discourage students from clinching, let each student wear a flag football belt. Sparring proceeds as normal for the round, with each flag grabbed from the partner's belt worth 2 or 3 points added to the final score.
    o **Protection Sparring** – This works especially well with families, but it can be used with a target or a person. Basically, sparring proceeds as normal with one person having to protect the target. If the opposing player kicks the target, he will win and the match will be over.

- o **Multiple Opponents** – Multiple opponent sparring is great to teach students to look out for everything happening around them. You will probably want to limit contact, however, as students can be hurt from blind attacks.
- o **Tag Team** – This concept has been more popular in tournaments lately. Only two players spar at a time, but students can signal (or touch) others to come in and spar for them. It leads to strategies to take advantage of mismatches, etc.
- o **Super Counters** – Have one person attack very slowly, and the other throw as many counters as possible in that time frame. Teaches them to react to chambers and body positions.
- o **Sudden Victory** – When you want to work on a specific technique, decide that the first person who does that technique well will win the match and the match will be over.

A comprehensive guide on how to spar is beyond the scope of this book, and varies depending on the martial art taught. However, here are a few important tips:

- **Encourage few techniques during matches, many during practice.** Remind your students that if they know 100 kicks and their opponent knows 98, it doesn't mean that they will win. It's the one technique they do at that instant vs. the one their opponent does that will determine who scores at that instant, and whoever scores more points will win. For example, a sloppy spinning back kick will likely get you scored on after you spin. However, other techniques should be tried in practices, so that they can be learned well enough to use in competition.

- **Recognize that sparring is about finding a way to win.** It will be rare that you will be taller, faster, more experienced, smarter, and better conditioned than your opponent. If so, the match is easy to win. However, usually you will have some advantages and some disadvantages. Maximize your advantages while minimizing your partner's. For instance, if no one can withstand your partner's attack, then you must always attack first. If your partner is fast but has bad endurance, keep the match close and then take advantage in the last round. A great spin hook kick will not help your opponent if you never give him a chance to throw it. Of course, to do this requires you to know the strengths and weaknesses of both your students and their opponents.

- **Competition is just a part of martial arts.** Don't encourage winning at the expense of your martial arts discipline, as often happens. Don't allow sparring to turn into fighting. Make sure your students always shake hands and congratulate the other competitor and coach, win or lose. Don't let sparring be a venue for personal revenge.

- **Scrimmage Often, and Analyze the Results.** You should face against other schools outside of competitions to see what is working in your training and what is not. Usually, other schools will want to face you as well. This is a friendly atmosphere and economically much more feasible than competing in tournaments.

For teaching grappling, many of the same rules apply, with some important exceptions. The injury rate during grappling is generally less than during sparring, even though little protective gear is worn. Also, children will naturally be more likely to jump right into grappling without fear. Chances are that they already grapple with their friends on the playground, and they will be excited to learn how to do it properly. However, some students, especially those who have undergone tragic experiences in the past, may be extremely hesitant to engage in any grappling. It is a commonly held belief that women do not like to grapple, however, in a survey in our school, females 13+ rated it their favorite activity out of 11, while males rated it second. Make sure you have policies that make sense for your school. For instance, boys and girls might grapple together, while males and females would not. Or, you might allow mixed grappling only for the women who consistently defeat the other women, or leave it up to the individual choice of both the woman and man. For instance, a man in a fragile marriage might not want to grapple another woman out of fear that his wife might get the wrong idea.

If your students are unsure about grappling, it will often help to acknowledge their fear and that it is perfectly natural. However, remind them that if they ever were attacked, that they will certainly feel nervous and uncomfortable. By also not feeling comfortable on the ground, they will give their attacker an extra advantage. The famous grappler Royce Gracie was asked why he didn't practice more takedown defense and he reportedly replied *"Why should a shark be scared to be pulled into the water?"* Let them know that they too could become a shark and give any would-be assailant a big surprise.

- **As with sparring, start slowly** – Work on basic positioning and drills before free grappling. At a very minimum, make absolutely sure all students know about tapping and how to avoid injury. Also, if starting from standing, make sure students are comfortable with their falling technique.

- **Teach positions first, then submissions** – Not only will this lead to less injuries, it will lead to better grapplers. Often beginners will focus too much on submissions, without their technical basics. Let students grapple only for points before you allow them to do submissions.

- **Don't allow all submissions** – Allowing only a subset of submissions will be safer and easier for students to really get the details down. Also, consider never allowing certain dangerous submissions (i.e., twisting knee locks, spine manipulations, etc.) You may need to practice these things for the tournaments you compete in, but in that case allow them only for advanced students.

- **Use mini-games** – Grappling lends itself to many mini games. If there is a clear winner and loser, let all the students line up from smallest to biggest, and progress through a bracket until you have a "class champion" who could be awarded with a free water, etc. after class. If there are widely differing sizes, split to two divisions.
  - **Arm Bar Game** – From the mount, one student tries to apply either a bent or straight arm arm bar. The other tries to defend, while the first tries to stop the defense, or chain to triangle, omaplata, arm bar from the guard, etc. This game could be played with almost any submission.
  - **Get to Mount Game** – From the guard, the person on the bottom tries to sweep while the person on top tries to pass. Let the low rank choose which position to occupy.
  - **Standing Control Game** – Let students start with one underhook, and try to lift their partner.

- o **Escape/Pass Etc. Game** – Give the students 10, 20, etc. seconds to escape the mount, or let both students be on top and see who can escape more quickly. Or, let all the students mount their partners and see who is the first in the class to escape.
- o **Double Leg Takedown Game** – Designate the student who will shoot, and then the other student will try to sprawl, get the back, half dump, etc. The shooter can go for double leg, single leg, ankle pick, etc. The winner is the one who ends up in the dominant position.
- o **Grapple the Ball** – This game is great for grappling skills. Have two people try to get a ball or other small object and bring it back to their side. This works best with submissions. If someone holds onto it with two hands it will be secure, but they will be open to chokes. If they hold on with one hand, they will be vulnerable to arm locks.
- o **Cliff Edge Game** – Let two people grapple in a small ring. You can win by submitting your partner or throwing them off the edge of the cliff. You stay in as long as at least one part of your body is in bounds.

In grappling, knowing a large number of techniques is more important than in sparring, because there are more techniques available and it is easier to catch someone with something they don't know. However, it's still better to know a few things well first.

Lesson 20: Teaching Combat

Teaching sport combat is great, but someone attacking your students on the street is not going to abide by competition rules. In some ways, all of the drills that we do have some relationship to sport combat, whether it is by conditioning, mental ability, or technique. However, practicing for real combat involves a different mindset and different techniques and combinations than you might ordinarily use.

Comprehensive System
The first thing you should do is analyze whether your system is comprehensive. There is no way to train for every possible situation that your students might encounter. However, they should in general be familiar with techniques that could work from different distances (from sliding kicks to grappling), techniques that can work against multiple opponents, and dealing with obstacles/uneven terrain.

Fundamental Problem
The fundamental problem of martial arts is that being good at anything requires practice, and fighting requires the ability to hurt your partner. How do you become good at fighting without hurting your partner in training? Many ideas in this book try to go around this principle from different angles.

It is imperative that you practice your techniques against a resisting partner. If your students have done a lot of free sparring and free grappling, then they should be well on their way. However, they still must train the two of them together. Let students put on all the sparring pads, but if they get a chance, they can take their partner down and grapple them. In order to keep this safe, there are several important things you will want to consider. You will probably want to limit contact, especially when on the ground or when one is on the ground and one standing. Depending on your sparring style, you may also have to add new pads, such as MMA training gloves. Regular MMA gloves are much too thin to do this safely.

You may want to have different "levels" of this type of training, where higher levels have more contact/target areas/submissions allowed. Another great way to add realism is to have two or more attackers face against one student.

Circle Drills

One of the most popular of all martial arts drills are the circle drills, where one person stands in the middle and the other students circle around him and then attack. There are many different variations to these drills. You could have each student on the outside have a number, and then when the instructor calls it, they attack. You can have students randomly choose to attack. You can have them all attack with a specific technique, or make up their own. You can have them all attack with a single technique, or combination.

You can have the people on the outside wearing pads or holding pads, or just have them not wear pads and have no contact. You can have multiple people attack at once, or just a single one.

Surprise Drills

In sport combat we all know who we are going to face (the guy on the other side of the ring wearing the pads) but in real life we have no such luxury. Have drills where a student will walk across the dojang and passing by other students, not knowing who will attack them. Reading an attacker's intentions quickly can give them the extra split second that they need to successfully counter. You might have no one attack the student, or a different number of people. The key is that the student doesn't know who will attack them or how many people will attack them.

Protection Drills

Martial arts is often talked about for self defense, but the defense of others must not be neglected. When a family is out and one is attacked, the most skilled have a responsibility to protect the others. Use a bag, BOB, or person to simulate the person being attacked. The student must defend himself and the other person as well.

A drill that we do that combines aspects of both of these is called "Bodyguard Training." One student is "Mr. President" and they have one or two bodyguards. They will shake hands with a line of people, not knowing that some of them will try to attack them or the President. If an attack occurs, they must get the President to a safe spot without him getting struck.

Lesson 21: Teaching Non-Physical Requirements

Physical requirements are only a part of what we are trying to teach our students. Non-physical requirements can roughly be broken down into the following categories:

- **Character Traits** – We want our students to be brave, loyal, humble, etc.

- **History and Tradition** – We want our students to understand and respect the origins of our school and art. We also want them to understand and appreciate cultural and linguistic aspects of our art's history.

- **Intelligent Decisions** – We want our students to make intelligent decisions in and out of the ring. This includes things like how to analyze an opponent, how to avoid trouble by avoiding poor choices, how to determine a strategy and select techniques to use, etc. We also want students who understand human physiology and the biomechanics of martial arts.

- **Intangibles** – Focus, concentration, creativity, and other traits can sometimes not be easily measured, but are still incredibly important.

Character traits will mostly be taught by example, by the way you interact with your students, instructors, and parents. Character traits are also taught during the normal process of training, especially if the right words are said at the right time. For example, a student who lost a match would need encouragement and to know the value of not giving up.

Character traits can also be taught by lecture or by focusing on a specific trait for a certain period of time. One suggestion is to use the "Word of the Month" lessons found at www.martial-arts-instructor-training.com. These lessons include specific tasks that you can choose to assign students to accomplish for each trait.

Teaching history and tradition is often accomplished by giving the students a book or handout in the beginning highlighting key facts.

Leading by example is very important here as well. If the master bows each time he enters the dojang, students will be much more likely to do it themselves. It is difficult to always be "on" but it is important for instructors to be examples of the traditional way they want their students to act.

One of the biggest keys to getting your students to use words and actions from a different language is to use them daily. Soon, your students will know these words as well as they know any in English. No one will say "let's go to the martial arts training hall" when they can just say "dojo." You might also add certain groups of words into your promotion test requirements and have an oral or written test. We have a disk with the files in MP3 format that we give to students when they start so that they can listen to them on their portable music players.

Other drills to help students learn terminology include:

- Give students a number in English, and then have them run back and forth. Call out a number in Korean and then they can spar, grapple, do forms, etc. If they don't remember their number and fail to come out within five seconds, their team loses that point.
- Sit in a circle and drill terminology as a way to have students rest from difficult conditioning practices.
- Encourage the students to make flashcards and drill them at home, or sell some pre-made ones in your proshop.
- Call out a technique in Korean and see which students are able to do it first.

When teaching history and tradition, stories are very important. Tell stories about your instructor, and their instructor. Even though times have changed, appropriate stories can still help the students get a sense of the past. Also, re-emphasize aspects of the training over and over, especially with children. Ask them questions such as *"Why do we bow before and after sparring?"* *"What's so special about this training area?"* or *"What does the school logo mean?"* Don't assume that your students will know these answers just because you taught them about it once.

To teach your students to become more intelligent, explain the purpose and mechanics of the drills that you do with them. You may also want to hold special seminars on areas of interest. Good decision making in the ring will come with experience and experienced coaches. This training is part of general sport combat training. If your students have good character traits, they will likely also make intelligent decisions. Finally, never neglect your own training. Take classes at a community college and read books to expand your own understanding. You can't teach your students things you don't know yourself.

Training intangibles is the most difficult of all. However, much will be gained through the structure of the class and belt curriculum. Honestly try to impart as much wisdom to your students as possible and you will have success here.

Lesson 22: Classroom Management

Classroom management is broadly defined as making sure everything in the classroom goes according to plan. This lesson will be shorter than the others, as most of the key points have been covered elsewhere. Let's reiterate some of the key points and also examine some new information.

When students are misbehaving in the class, refer to the lesson on discipline and punishment. Before they misbehave, however, try to set up your classroom and lesson plans to take away their opportunities to misbehave.

- **Avoid Distractions** – If the beginners line up so that they are staring out the window to a busy street, you might have a problem. If the kids who always climb on the heavy bags line up right next to where they are stored, you might have a problem. Set up your class so that children will have as few opportunities to be distracted as possible.

- **Face Away from Parents** – If children are looking "through" you to their parents, you will only reach them with limited information.

- **Use Appropriate Groupings** – If your class is larger than about 8 students or has students who need to learn different things, split them into groups and let them each work with an assistant instructor. It's best to do a warm-up and other drills together in a large group, and then later split into small groups for rank-specific instruction.

- **Use Time Out** – If a student's misbehavior is affecting or endangering other students, put him in time out until he is ready to come back and participate. We must always try our best for *every* student, but remember that sometimes spending all your time on 1 student in class will cause you to lose the other 29.

- **Vary the Drills** – Sometimes you will get the feeling of something the class is missing. Perhaps their energy is low, or maybe they're too fidgety. Learn to recognize this and change a drill to bring the class back on track.

- **Zero Down Time** – Try to set up drills ahead of time, but if you are by yourself, give the students something to do while you work. For example, *"Everyone give me 10 laps while I set up the agility ladder."*

- **Have Appropriate Supervision** – Depending on the level and age of the students, make sure you have enough instructors. You need more instructors for younger students. Sometimes, you may have to cap off the class even if you have enough instructors.

Lesson 23: Games

Games are an important part of your teaching technique arsenal. Why? Because people always try harder when it's a competition. Ask someone to run a lap, and then ask again and tell them you're timing it. Competition increases effort, and for most students, it's fun as well.

The main reason we enter tournaments is not to win more medals. It's so that our students can be pushed to their limits and increase what they thought they were capable of. There are, of course, dangers to competition. Most of these dangers will manifest in a tournament setting, not in relay races to warm up the class.

The main danger of using games in class is that parents may say something like *"We're not paying for him to do what he can do on the playground for free."* This is an important point. Although playtime is very necessary for kids, most kids will have playtime outside of martial arts class. To make sure your games aren't perceived this way, here are a few important tips.

- **Explain the purpose** – If parents and students know that this drill is to work on their reaction time, or their agility, etc. they'll be less likely to think of it as wasted time.

- **Use Appropriate Terminology** – Is something a game or a drill? For children, nearly everything can be called a 'game' while for adults it can be called a 'drill.' For instance, kicking a bag can be "In this game, let's see who can show me the best roundhouse kick!" Little children may try harder when they think it's a game. All games are drills. A drill is just an exercise you do to teach some skill; thus games are a type of drill, and it could be appropriate to call something either one.

- **Winners and Losers** – Many games, including the one listed above, may not have a clear winner, or you may not announce one. If they press you, ask *"Who had fun and learned something?"* When everyone raises their hands, say *"Then you're all the winners!"* The point of the game is not to get winners and losers, the point is to make everyone try harder. Other games will have clear winners and losers.

For the most part, this isn't a problem, but some sensitive students (especially young kids) will start to feel sad if they never win. If the game allows it, have multiple rounds. Nothing makes someone forget his disappointment over not winning like having another chance. Also, never stigmatize the losers. For instance, in a game with multiple teams, if the losers receive 10 pushups, tell the winning teams that they are allowed to do pushups too, either in support of their friends or to make sure others don't train more than them.

- **Change Winning Criteria** – Let the winning criteria reflect what you want to accomplish. If people are doing pushups too fast, reward the one with the slowest pushups. Reward the one with the highest squat jumps or the least fidgets during class. This is a great way to get students to focus on whatever you need them too. You could have different rounds, for instance with a form. In the first round, reward the best stances, second best chambers, third most power, and last, loudest kihap. This is also a great way to disguise repetition.

- **School Records Board** – It can be helpful to have a board with the 'school records' in various events, broken down by gender and age (and perhaps rank as well.) List records for whatever is important to you, i.e., most kicks in 10, 30, 60 seconds, highest jumping kick, most continuous nunchuck backspins, etc. Every once in a while hold a 'school Olympics' in class or for a special event and let students try to break the records and get their name and the date on the board.

- **Keep it in Focus** – Remind the students that the only true competition in martial arts is with themselves. This is where the school records board, or at least quantifying results, will come in handy. Most students will not set a school record, but they can set a personal record in any of the events. Let them see improvement, and they will be motivated to keep working hard.

Here are some specific games for use in martial arts classes:

- **Statue Game** – In this game let the students run around and 'go crazy' for a few seconds before you shout 'attention.' If any of the students move, make them sit down. Go through your basic postures, and when a student is the last one standing, they win! If everyone makes it, everyone can be the winner. If the students who had to sit down sit perfectly still, let them get another chance to come back into the game. Works best with 3-6 year old children.

- **Relay Races** – Line the students up in teams and run relays. The races can be simple races (i.e., running, kicking, crawling, shrimping, etc.) or you can have them run down and do something (falling technique, form, etc.). Other fun variations require students to run and jump over an obstacle (flying side kick, roll, or freestyle), or carry equipment back and forth.

- **Choreographed Fight Scene** – Have the students get together and choreograph a sparring match or fighting scene. See how creative they get, and then you can pick the best one!

- **Extended Snake Race** – With a line of students, have the first kneel down and the second jump over, and then kneel down. The third jumps over the first two and kneels, until they reach the last person. Then, the last comes through. You could also do this with leapfrog, or weaving over and under. You could have the students lie on their backs and lift their legs, and alternatively (be careful) have them lightly step on each other's stomachs.

- **Kicking Relays** – There are several ways to do kicking relays. You could have each team do 500 kicks, and let them decide how many each person would do each time. Also, for continuous double kicks, have one person keep kicking until he breaks rhythm or gets tired, and then the next one comes up. The last team still kicking is the winner. Alternatively, have the first person kick once, the second twice, etc. up to 10 or 15 and then back down again.

- **Ball Game** – This is a favorite. Instead of dodge ball where two teams face each other across a line, make a square with an inside team and outside team. The outside team will roll/throw balls at the inside team. The key is that the inside team will learn to be aware of everything happening around them. For added difficulty, let the inside team only crawl/roll out of the way. Works best with large exercise balls.

- **Paddleball** – A time honored traditional game for Taekwondo schools, this involves two teams with goals on the opposite sides of the dojang. With a small ball of tape, each team must hit the ball into the opposing team's goal. You can wear hogus and allow some pad to person contact if desired.

- **Reaction Ball Game** – Using a multi-lobed reaction ball (such as is used for training soccer goalies) have lines stand behind you. When you yell *"GO!"* throw two balls and let the students run and chase them. Whoever brings their ball back to you first is the winner. For added difficulty, add obstacles that they must jump over/crawl under before you throw their ball.

- **Ring Toss Game** – Throw an agility ring in the air and make the students run forward and punch through the middle. For extra difficulty, go farther away, or throw multiple rings at a time. Vary the angle of the ring if you want students to change to kicks, uppercuts, etc. Works great with a bo staff or sword as well. Another variation is to have one student, and throw several rings at him, forcing him to react and run around the room to retrieve them.

- **Form Moves Game** – A great way to teach forms is to have the students come up one at a time and run through their form from the beginning. Give them one point for each move they do correctly, and 'beep' them as soon as they make a mistake. Thus someone who made a mistake on the fifth move would have four points. This will really help them focus on correcting their mistakes that they might have just blown off before. You can change how strict you are or give our 'bonuses' if they finish the whole thing. For example, there could be a '5 point chambering bonus' or '5 point power bonus.' You could also allow them one or two 'lifelines' where you will correct their errors or they can ask their friends for help.

- **Add on Combinations Game** - This one works with forms, hand techniques, kicking, or weapons. One student does the first move, and then the second does the move that the first one did and then adds his own. The third does what the first two did and then adds his own.

When a student forgets the combo, he is out. Keep going until someone can't remember or can't do the move.

- **Stances Game** – One way to make sure the students' stances are stable is to have them face each other and try to off balance each other. This works particularly well with long stance. It's easy to sacrifice, but if you step or fall, you lose, even if your partner does it first.

- **Balance Balls Game** – Using balance balls, you can have the students stand on one and see who can stand on one leg the longest. Also, you can have them stand on one and see how many kicks they can do without falling off, or have them stand on two and try to block attacks or projectiles until they fall off.

- **Sabumnim/Sensei Says** – Like Simon Says. This one works well because students are used to reacting to your hard commands.

- **Taekwondo Tag** – Have the students tag each other (better to have 2 people for large classes) and have them tag the others. The others would then have to do pushups, sit-ups, crane stance for 10 seconds, etc. to be free. You could also have the person tagging count in Korean, or say the name of a block, punch, etc. when tagging.

- **Aerial Pad Game** – Throw pads at them and have the students strike them out of the air. Make sure to use pads without hard spots, like square hand mitts. You can see if they do it correctly by the trajectory that the pad takes after the strike. You could also have rewards for hitting certain targets. Depending on your training space, you might want to do this one outside.

- **Square Team Sprint Game** – Divide the students into two teams and make a square in the middle. Line them up at opposite corners of the square. When you say go, the first person from each team runs to try to catch the other one. If they make it all the way around, they can then tag their team and the second person will take over. For more difficulty, make the square smaller and have them run around it more than once.

- **Slow Pushup Contest** – A great way to work on pushups technique is to have a contest where they must do pushups as slowly as possible, but never stop. Give them only ten or so pushups to do, and the last one to finish is the winner. Make sure they count out loud to discourage cheating.

- **Timed Obstacle Course** – Obstacle courses are great training for classes where there aren't too many students. If there are more, have them all go through it at the same time. If less, let one go through it at a time and time her. An added bonus of this type of game is that the student will have everyone cheering for her, which some kids have never experienced outside of martial arts.

- **Groups Games** – If your class isn't giving you good energy, simply face the two halves of the class towards each other and do the drill again. This time, see which half has the higher kicks, louder yells, better stances, etc. Your intensity will increase.

- **Mirror Game** – Have one student do any action, and the other has to read the action and react as fast as possible. It could be specific such as using only footwork and one person always tries to keep it in open or closed stance, or it could be completely general, allowing any human action.

- **Shoulder Sparring** – In this game the students try to touch each other on the shoulder without allowing their partner to touch them. Be careful they don't hit in the face. This game will encourage the development of strategy, reaction time, and faking/trapping skills.

- **Foot Step Game** – Similar to the game above, have each student try to lightly step on their partner's foot.

- **High Kick/Five/Roll Game** – Line the students up and have them come one at a time to kick/ high five/ dive roll onto a big pad. If everyone makes it through the round, raise the target for the next round. Since the students will be running and jumping with a lot of speed and height, make sure you have the proper padding.

- **Blocking Game** – Use a pool noodle or foam sword to attack from different angles and force the students to react and block. Kids will love it if you add an 'impossibility round' where you go extremely fast with two simultaneous angles of attack. You can also have them try to block after/during a kick, punch, or roll.

- **Block/Fall/Jump Game** – Take two foam swords and have two students at a time run at you. When they are almost there, you do either a vertical strike (they must do high block) a high horizontal strike (they must do falling technique to avoid) or a low horizontal strike (they must jump). They will love trying to react on time.

- **Longest Combo/Double Kicks Game** – You will likely need a park for this one. See how long they can do continuous double kicks, or see who can do the longest combination of kicks before stopping.

- **Double kicks race** – Have the students lay down next to the kicking bag in several teams. When you call a number, they have to jump up, do that many kicks, and then get back down. The last person in the line is eliminated, and one person from his team must come forward to take his spot. Each team will become eliminated until there is only one left. You might also want to put the low ranks in the front because otherwise one fast person can defeat the whole class and the other people on his team won't get a turn. You can do variations of having them sit facing away/towards the bag or lying down.

- **Baseball** – You can play baseball with a large ball and have the students kick it. This one would work best at the park. Alternatively, you could use weapons as well but be careful.

- **Pick a Technique Challenge** – Works especially well with forms or other requirements. Have two teams, and when a person from one team comes up they get to challenge the other team with any technique. Both of them do that technique, and the one who does it better wins (either that person to be on their team, or a point.) This is good for getting students to remember their previous forms.

- **Take the Pad** – Have the students line up on either side of the room, and put muy thai or square pads in the middle, 2 less than the number of students. Have each student run and try to get a pad. If two people go for the same pad, you can grapple to take it away. If time is called, whoever has the dominant position will win, as long as they are both touching the pad. This will stop them from trying to just lay down on it.

- **Color Game** – For small kids, put several objects out in the room. Then when you yell a color, they all have to run and touch something that is of that color. It's a fun way to get them working hard.

- **Steal The Bacon** – In this game two students will come forward and try to get an object. You can play with several variations. They can either get it and bring it back, or tag their partner if they have it. Also, you can have them grapple their partner to take it as well.

- **Fastest Kick** – Set two teams (people) up on either side of a bag. Make sure they start the same distance apart. On your signal, they both have to kick with their same leg (to avoid clashing). Whoever kicks first wins.

- **Blaster Pad Sparring** – This one is very popular and was used as a stand alone event at our school tournament in 2009. Two people face each other in a small ring. You can only attack your partner with your shield, and you win by knocking him down or out of the ring.

- **Sparring Games** – See the section on sparring for more information on how you can modify sparring with different types of games.

- **Grappling Games** – See the section on grappling for more info about various grappling mini-games.

Lesson 24: Special Students

Dealing with Challenging Children/Learning Disabilities

You will have a wide variety of children in your classes. Some will listen perfectly to everything you say, whereas others will seem to willfully disobey. Many children will seem like they genuinely want to pay attention, but at the first slight distraction will lose focus. There is a good chance that some of these children will have **Attention Deficit/Hyperactivity Disorder (ADHD).** It is estimated that ADHD affects approximately 5% of all American children. However, because of the therapeutic effects of martial arts, the percentage of ADHD in our students is probably much higher. Many of the cases in our students may not be officially diagnosed. Here are some symptoms of ADHD

- Problems taking turns
- Going from one uncompleted activity to another
- Difficulty being quiet. They will often play in a loud voice.
- Talks excessively.
- Does not seem to listen
- Takes many risks
- Difficulty with handwriting
- Poor eye contact
- Decreased coordination
- Less mature than same age peers.

Here are some of the ways that ADHD may affect learning

- Children fidget constantly
- Children are very easily distracted
- Children are impulsive
- Children may procrastinate
- Children may have difficulty with timed tasks
- Children may be forgetful
- Children may hear/understand only part of what you have said.

ADHD is a neurological problem dealing with chemicals in the brain. The brains of ADHD children use glucose at a slower rate than normal. The cause is currently unknown, although there is a strong genetic link. Almost 60% of parents with ADHD will have a child with ADHD.

Autism Spectrum Disorder (Aspergers/Autism)

Autism is a disorder where children have a profound difficulty relating to the outside world. Thus, it is often hard for them to have many friends or engage in "normal" activities. They may have difficulty understanding other people's feelings or their point of view. Also, they may become fixed on one particular aspect or subject.

Autistic children are rare in class because it is often difficult for them to function at a level high enough to understand that there is a class going on or what their place in it is.

Aspergers is more common, as these children can often function in the class. Many Aspergers children are in fact very bright. They may do well in school, and may be able to memorize something like an entire movie after seeing it only once. However, they may have problems differentiating between a class and a movie or video game. Often, these students will become very 'into' Taekwondo.

Tourette's Syndrome

Between one and ten in one thousand people have some form of Tourette's syndrome, although many cases are not diagnosed because the symptoms are mild. Tourette's is commonly thought to be a disease where people are prone to sudden uncontrollable and inappropriate outbursts, but this is true only in a minority of cases. The most common symptoms are 'ticks' or sudden involuntary muscle spasms. Students may also always have to rub their hands together or make a similar motion.

Other Learning Disabilities

Our brains and bodies perform thousands of functions, and a defect in any one could lead to a separate disorder. Some could be straightforward— for instance, if a child had a hearing disability, the instructor might only have to talk louder. Some could be more complicated and not even understood by researchers. Some other examples could include students who have abnormal trouble remembering things, students who cannot differentiate between right and left or right and wrong, students who have trouble controlling their muscle or nerve function, etc. However, this is not a psychology or biology textbook, so we won't go into everything. The important thing to know is how to work with these students so they can get all the benefits of martial arts training.

Teaching Strategies

Remember, we are not doctors, and it is not our job to say who has ADHD or anything else. However, we can still implement several teaching strategies to help these children. Sometimes, your most rewarding moments as an instructor will come from making progress with these children.

- **Reduce Distractions** – If possible, try not to have two easily distractible children next to each other, as they will end up distracting each other. If possible, have them in smaller classes with less noise from parents, other students, traffic, etc.
- **Give Short, Direct Commands** – If you give a long rambling command, the student will have forgotten the first part by the time you get to the end.
- **Teach Information in Smaller, More Manageable Chunks** – Teach 4 or 6 moves at a time, instead of the whole form.
- **Don't Pre-judge** – These kids are often labeled 'problem kids' from school or their peers. Let them know that they have a clean slate with you. As teachers, we have to believe in all of our students. It may take a while, but you'll find the untapped potential within.
- **Develop Rapport** – Many of these kids have few actual friends. While it is not your job to be their friend, respecting you and knowing that you are their friend will make them more receptive to you.
- **Keep Your Temper/ Don't Ridicule Them** – Although you might want to pull out your hair, this will only make things worse. For instance, one time I was giving a promotion test, and a student threatened to give me pushups! Although this would have caused a

normal student to fail, I simply reminded this person that that wasn't the way it works.
- **Be Careful With Discipline** – If you say *"The next person that moves in Choombie owes 50 pushups"* and they move, you have to give them the pushups. Otherwise, they will test you more. Make sure your discipline is consistent and in line with the crime.
- **Catch Them Doing Something Good** – Sometimes, these children will act up just to get attention. Praising them for the things that they do well will alleviate this problem. Also, sometimes it is hard to find a great technique worthy of a compliment- in this case, praise effort or progress. Give a lot of small steps and give encouragement as they reach each one.
- **Be Specific and Positive** – Saying *"Keep your leg straight"* instead of *"Don't bend your knee"* will help reinforce the right way and give less room for misinterpretation.
- **Reinforce Structure** – If a kid says *"I want to play a game"* remind him who is in charge. Remind them that no matter how they act outside the dojang, inside 'Your House" there are rules that they have to follow if they want to remain a student.
- **Be PATIENT**- Above all, it will take a longer time, but the students will learn. Practice basics repeatedly.

"Be tender with the young, compassionate with the aged, sympathetic with the striving and tolerant of the weak and strong. Because someday in your life you will have been all of these."

George Washington Carver

Lesson 25: Discipline and Punishment

Discipline is often thought of as punishment, but a better definition is doing what you should do when you don't want to, or doing what's right when it's easier to do what's wrong.

One of the main goals of martial arts training is to use external discipline on undisciplined students in a way that leads to internal discipline. That means the instructor must discipline the students until the students can discipline themselves.

Self discipline is always preferable to external discipline for several reasons, including the fact that the instructor isn't with the students 24 hours a day, seven days a week. Also, self discipline can be stronger than external discipline and extend into more areas of life. So how do you get people to be self disciplined?

- Show them the way. If you are self disciplined, you should have achieved numerous desirable things in your life. Maybe it's a good roundhouse kick, a stable livelihood, or a good marriage. People look up to you. Students will see this and want to pattern their lives after you. Use your influence.
- The structure of the school will help as well. The various high belts should be closer to these things than the various low belts. Point it out, in a proper way. You might say, "Master Kamil didn't go to sleep one night overweight and wake up with a six pack. He did x number of sit-ups every day for 2 years, even when he was tired."
- Recognize examples of good self-discipline, such as straight A students, people who always keep their room clean, etc.
- Encourage students to think about the reasons certain actions are 'right' or desirable, and 'wrong' or undesirable. This isn't generally in a moral sense, but more in a sense of why each quality benefits or doesn't benefit the school. For instance, you could have a school with or without respect, which one would they prefer? If they were sparring someone, would they prefer that that person lose their temper or not?

- Discipline Check List. Give students a list to take home that includes tasks such as cleaning their rooms, making their beds, taking out the trash, etc.

Punishment

There are many images of masters yelling "*100 pushups on your knuckles!*" But how effective is this? In short, punishment is used to stop a negative behavior. In the old days, pretty much anything was accepted as punishment. Masters would hit students, often with a "spirit stick," shinai, or other weapon. Many would also come up with more creative punishments, including standing for long periods of time in horse stance, doing the master's yard work, working with the white belts, etc. Sometimes, the master would just beat the student up in sparring.

Many of these things are in fact, illegal, especially hitting the students. Others might possibly, though not likely, be seen as illegal work, i.e., something that only an employee should be doing. That's not to say that creative punishment doesn't have its place, as it certainly does. One punishment administered at our school involved an 11 year old girl who had taken a couple of dollars out of the cash register to buy candy. The punishment involved her writing an essay about why what she did was wrong to read in front of the class.

Be careful about going back on your word. In the above case, the girl was mortified of the assignment and terrified of what her fellow classmates would think. In this case, she was required only to write the essay and turn it in, not read it in front of the class. If you go back on your word on punishments, then students will think that you're not serious about them, or that punishments are negotiable. Do so only in the most extreme cases, and only when you are absolutely convinced that the student has learned her lesson.

Punishment can have some negative consequences as well. It might be okay to embarrass a student slightly, but students should never be humiliated. For instance, telling a student "Don't eat your belt" when they're supposed to be standing at attention is not going to harm the student, but would cause them to avoid that specific behavior in the future. If the punishment is painful, or humiliating, or scary, it might cause the student to drop out. Also, if you have several instructors who apply punishment in different ways, it might cause students to act differently around different instructors. Certainly, different instructors might have different styles and personalities, but if people are only acting good for one instructor, then they aren't internalizing their discipline.

Punishment as Training.

Probably the most common punishment in the martial arts is pushups. However, pushups are also part of normal training. If students are told to do pushups, how do they know if they've been acting badly or not? While some instructors see this as a dilemma, the instructor should make the purpose of the pushups clear to everyone. Using punishments as training also has the benefit of making the students stronger. Thus while these punishments take time out of the drill, the time isn't wasted. Students may be more willing to do punishments that they see as still helping their training.

Group vs. Single Punishment

Many experts might question punishing someone for someone else's behavior, but that can be important in building a team atmosphere. It could also be someone's responsibility to stop that behavior. For instance, a master has to go into the office to talk to someone, and a black belt is stretching while several white belts are sparring without pads. It is the black belt's responsibility to tell the white belts to stop. The school is a family atmosphere. Thus, if most of the class is talking, the whole class can get ten pushups. This is especially important if it's a 'team' atmosphere, such as a competition team. Sometimes you can punish everyone but the troublemaker. If someone is not modifying their behavior, let the rest of the class do ten pushups while they count for them.

Suggested Punishments – Here are a few suggested punishments, in relative order of severity.

Verbal Reprimand – Tell the students what they are doing wrong, and why. This is often the first stage. Another option that is less a punishment is to complement the desired behavior in another student. For example, thanking the five people who are sitting correctly will help the ones who are not sitting correctly to modify their behavior.

Physical Punishment – Pushups, situps, etc.

Time Out – If a student is disrupting a class, let them sit out for a few minutes. Time out during a game is far more effective than time out during something the student dislikes.

Loss of Belt/Status/etc. – A more serious, though still temporary, punishment is to take the student's belt, kick them off the competition team, stop them from coming to weapons class, remove them as a member of the instructor training program, etc.

Removal From School – A final punishment would be only for the extreme cases where someone so seriously disrupts the class or endangers the other students that you cannot have the person a part of the school any longer. In such a case, it is also possible that the student should be reported to the police or could also endanger the general public. For extremely serious actions, i.e., murder, rape, abuse, theft, etc., the state takes over the primary responsibility for punishment from the school.

Other punishments that could work include forcing a student to pay for equipment or other items he destroyed, writing essays on why a given action was harmful, practicing a good action repeatedly. For instance, someone who forgets to bow when entering the school could enter and leave correctly ten times, etc.

When the student's actions involve hurting another person, it's almost always imperative that the student also apologize. An apology usually won't be the only punishment, but it shows that there are no hard feelings.

Punishment for Actions outside of Class/Tournament/Etc.
Some would say that we are only responsible for behavior that happens in our classroom, but that is at odds with our goal of providing complete personal development. Make it clear to parents that while it is primarily their job to raise their kids, you are their partner. Kids know that their parents have to love them, but you don't have that same requirement. Many parents find it helpful to bring serious discipline problems to the attention of the master, with better results than if they handled it themselves. A kid might clean up his room a bit better if he knows that you are going to come over and check it

sometime in the next two weeks. While this can be a big demand on your time, a little can also go a long way.

Other notes:

- **Punishments should be appropriate** – The nature and severity of a punishment should always match what the student did to deserve it.
- **Let them know that you care about them** – Students should know that you are punishing them because you want them to help improve their self-discipline. They should know that it's not personal, and that it doesn't mean that you don't like or care about them as a person.
- **Punish immediately** – Make sure that the person corresponds the punishment with the action, and stop the action.
- **Have standard punishments** – If everyone knows that it's 30 pushups to be late, there should be no resentment with it.
- **Punish the same** – If the same people do the same action, they should receive the same punishment, otherwise you may be accused of playing favorites. However, you must also take into account the age and belt of a student.
- **Work with parents** – For that are children, work with their parents. However, be careful of the point above, and also just because a parent wants something, doesn't make it right. For instance, several parents have let it be known that old school discipline is okay for their kids, but that doesn't make it right.
- **Punishing Instructors** – Instructors should refrain from punishing other instructors. That should only be done by the head instructor, and only in private.

Lesson 26: Legal Issues

Avoiding Negligence

Negligence and lawsuits are one of the scariest parts of training. If someone gets hurt in your class, they can sue you, and even press criminal charges against you. This can seem ridiculous, because everyone knows that martial arts is combat training, and there will be injuries.

Also, all it takes is one incident and one jury to start a precedent. For instance, in a famous case, McDonalds was sued for millions of dollars because someone spilled hot coffee on her lap. Now, you would think that someone buying hot coffee would expect their coffee to be hot, and not blame the people who sold her the hot coffee. However, now there are warning labels on all sorts of restaurant goods.

Negligence means that you had a duty to do something (as an instructor) and didn't do it. Basically, you 'should have' done something but you didn't.

The good news is that most schools have a corporate structure, insurance, liability waivers, and instructor training to help protect both instructors and the school from lawsuits and prosecution. Most schools are incorporated as a Limited Liability Company (LLC) or subchapter S Corporation. These designations provide a corporate shield so that assets held outside of the corporation are protected against lawsuits against the corporation.

However, it is also important to remember that anyone *can sue anyone for any reason*. For instance, in business, oftentimes a larger company will try to force a smaller company either to go out of business or delay a product launch and lose a competitive advantage by filing a lawsuit against them. The small company may not have enough resources to fight the suit and still bring their product to market first. There have even been cases of times when a criminal broke into a business and injured himself, and then sued the business for unsafe conditions! Often, a lawsuit is just an attempt to settle out of court. 95% of cases settle out of court.

The most important way to protect yourself is this: If no accidents occur, there can be no legitimate claims!

A key idea in the issue of negligence is that of 'accepted risk.' Thus, if someone chooses to train in Taekwondo, they have accepted a certain risk and cannot blame you for an injury. However, the critical point is that the instructor should do nothing to add to the risk. Doing so is negligence. In Bushnell v. Japanese-American Religious & Cultural Center, (1996) 43 Cal.App.4th (a judo black belt broke a white belt's leg during practice) the court found that the plaintiff did not even have a civil right to sue. Part of the opinion stated that *"liability should not be imposed simply because an instructor asked the student to take action beyond what, with hindsight, is found to have been the student's abilities. To hold otherwise would discourage instructors from requiring students to stretch, and thus to learn, and would have a generally deleterious effect on the sport as a whole."*

In another lawsuit, Wells v. Colorado College, (10th Cir. 1973) 478 F.2d 158 the plaintiff was injured when she fell directly onto the hardwood floor. The instructor failed to check the mats for safety and they separated in the middle of class. The court allowed this student to sue because the instructor's negligence had increased the inherent risks to the student.

So, in summary, if you do not intend harm or act recklessly and take adequate precautions, you can be protected somewhat if a lawsuit occurs.

There are three main dangers we need to avoid.

Training Area Dangers

These are things like torn mats, weapons lying around, cleaning chemicals in the reach of children, lack of visibility (i.e., office person cannot see training area), sharp objects on floor, things that might fall on someone, bad lighting, etc.

Training Equipment Dangers

Nunchucks with frayed rope, cracked weapons, sharp weapons in reach of children, heavy bags that might fall, pads that are too thin so all force goes right through them, etc.

Also, **make sure all students wear their full gear for sparring!**

Training Technique Dangers

Injuries will happen. The key thing is if you did something that made the injury more likely, i.e., if the person could have got the same benefit with a safer way. For instance, students shouldn't do dive rolls until they can safely do regular rolls. They shouldn't dive over 4 pads until they can dive over 3. Don't throw a student who can't fall. Look for things like:

Little kids holding bags for adults, too much contact/no control in sparring, traffic areas near weapons areas, beginning students holding pads in front of their face, students consistently using illegal techniques in a match, submission techniques practiced at full force, etc.

Also, students are required to 'mitigate' their own risk. For example, if a student with a bad knee keeps trying to do plyometrics, then the injury is his fault if he did not tell you about it. However, if he did say that he had a bad knee and asked to stop, and you didn't let him, then you will be in trouble. **Never push a student where he does not want to go because of an injury or other condition**. Of course, you must push the students, but if they reasonably ask not to do a drill, always let them substitute it with another drill. There is some exception with a minor, say a kid who never wants to do pushups but his dad says "*my son must do pushups!*" This should only be in case of general reluctance, not because of injury. If an instructor "bullies" or ridicules a student into doing the drill, then the student no longer has an assumed risk.

Always fill out incident reports immediately after an accident, and report any accidents directly to the head instructor. Also, in this case, do not speak with any press. Simply state that you are not authorized to speak to the media. Another important thing to note is that the school and owner can be sued for something his employees do. This might not seem fair, but that is the law. Owners are responsible for making sure everything in their school is being run according to generally accepted standards.

Sexual Abuse Liability

One of the scariest kinds of legal problems instructors could find themselves in is if there is any accusation of sexual abuse. It is recommended that school owners review every area of their operations with an attorney to minimize the chance that there could be any abuse and also the chance that there could be any false accusations. Here are a few suggestions to take into account:

- **Witnesses**- One of the biggest defenses is always having witnesses present. This can be other adult staff members, parents, other students, etc. Most schools also have an 'open door policy' stating that anyone is welcome to drop in unannounced at any time to observe class. An unscrupulous person looking for a quick payday will have trouble fabricating a case if there are always many people in the school.

- **Waivers/Student Agreements** – Schools should have a standard form that new students must fill out spelling out the conditions of the training offered. It can be helpful here to insert clauses stating that some martial arts techniques (i.e., grappling, groin strikes, etc.) could be perceived to be of a sexual nature but the student recognizes that they are part of normal training. You might also want to insert a clause that says students can always request a change of partner for any of these drills or request to do them with a dummy or training bag.

- **Instructor Background** – School owners should make sure that they know the backgrounds of any instructors that they hire.

Lesson 27: Parents

If you are teaching children, you will deal with their parents at some point. If you don't, then there is something wrong. You're violating the first point in dealing with parents!

- **Have a relationship** - It's important to have a relationship with as many of the parents as possible. This way, you are on the same page regarding what they want their children to get out of the program and how things are progressing. Remember, it is important that the parent sees you as an ally in working with their children.

- **Recognize that you want the same things** - Parents want their kids to be good at TKD, confident, do well in school, have positive friends, etc. When it seems like a parent is 'against' you, remember that you both have the same goals. Sometimes you might disagree on how to get there, but remember what you both want. Explain how your point of view will help out their child, and they will understand. Sometimes, it doesn't hurt to remind them that that is what is important to you.

- **Treat their individual issues as the most important to you** - You might have 100 students, but they have only one child. What's best for 90% of the kids doesn't interest them if their kid is one of the other 10%. Although they probably do genuinely care about the other students, they're going to act in what they perceive to be the best interests of their own children.

- **Listen to their questions** - By listening to what they're asking you, you can see what is important to them. When a parent of a Little Tigers student asks *"What's the youngest division in a tournament,"* they might really be asking *"When can my son compete in a tournament?"* If someone asks if the classes are large, they might really be asking how they can be sure their daughter will get enough individual attention. Listen to what they ask, look for non-verbal cues, and see how they respond to your answers. Don't be afraid to ask them *"What do you think about. ...?"* If you're not sure why they asked something, return the question with *"Is that important to you?"*

It will get you to see why they asked it.

- **Ask your own questions** - Frequently ask parents how their child is doing in school, with home issues, etc. This helps your relationship, but you have to be on top of things. You can't say "I hope he keeps up the good work in school!" when the kid is pulling in all Fs. See how he likes his training, if he wants to come to other classes, i.e. weapons, demo, etc.

- **Remember that YOU are the teacher**- it's great when parents want to be involved, but every once in a while you'll have a parent who's super-involved. They may critique their child and others, watch every class, or try to offer up training drills. One parent should never discipline the kids of another parent, only instructors should enforce discipline. I once had a parent repeatedly tell me how to run the class. We'd do forms and this parent would say *"We need to do more sparring."* We'd do sparring and it was *"How come we never do forms?"* It got to the point that I had to ask *"If you know so much more about training than me, why are you paying us to bring your child here?"* If a parent honestly believes that he or she can train their kid better than you, then they are wasting their money.

- **Use volunteers appropriately** - Parent volunteers can be a great source of help for a school, and many of them will be more than happy to help year after year. In our community at KAT, we've had floor installers, drywallers, computer technicians, painters, doctors, nurses, school principals, and professional athletes. This gives us a tremendous resource to help make the students better. However, beware of parents who seem a little 'too eager' to help. For instance, one new parent was so excited his kids were training. During the first week he said, *"Master Bill, KAT is so great! Let me know whatever you need, and I'll do it. I mean whatever. If the bathroom is dirty, I'll go clean it right now!"* Although I was happy to have such an enthusiastic person on board, within two months he blew up at another parent, withdrew his kids from the school, and several weeks later had a major heart attack. After he recovered, I met him one day in the store and he was much calmer.

- **Ask Parents to Train** - Parents who are often at the school have likely thought about training themselves. Once they start, it is usually a positive thing for their families. Remind them that we have many successful parent-students and that they usually are here anyway. Families who join together are also more likely to have successful outcomes to their training.

- **Watch a Class** – Watch a class from the point of view of a parent. Spend your time focusing on just one kid. What does that tell you? Is he listening? Did he do something wrong and not get correction from the instructor?

Handling Complaints from Students and Parents

You will have students and parents complain about some way that you run your class. The key is not to become too defensive up front. Oftentimes, they just want to be heard. Using the following steps can be very helpful.

1) **Listen**- Listen very thoroughly to the student or parent. Ask questions to get at the deeper root and so that they know you understand. Often, the real issue may not be what they first bring up. Don't argue with them. Let them "get it off their chest."
2) **Take Responsibility** – Even if it's their fault, there's probably something you did/didn't do that made them feel this way. State your desire to find an optimum solution. Thank them for bringing the problem to your attention.
3) **State Your Opinion** – Clear up any misconceptions that they have, and let them know your/the school's viewpoint.
4) **Agree on a Solution** – See what you can do to make them feel better. See Service Recovery as well.
5) **Follow Through** – You must make it a high priority to make sure it gets done.

Lesson 28: Body Planes and Motions

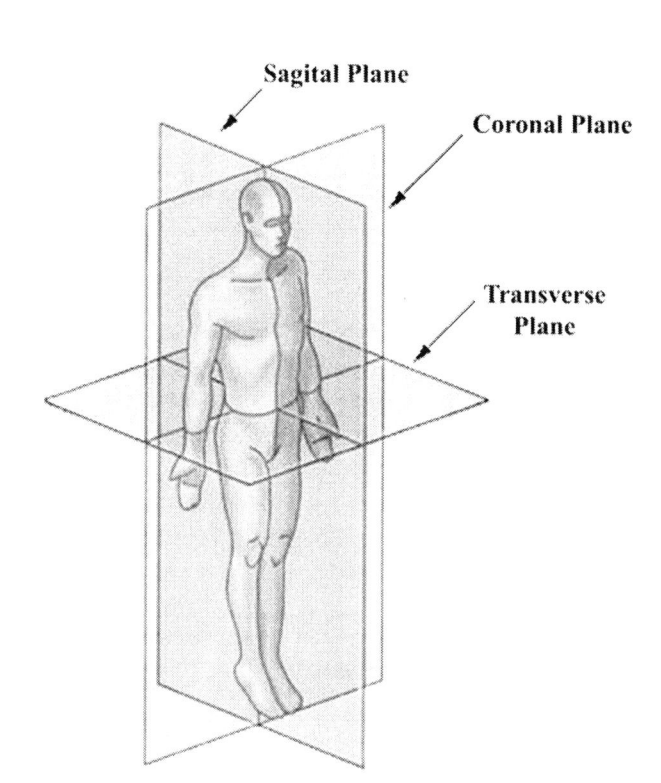

There are several technical terms for body motion used in science.

These motions are all in reference to the 3 main body planes illustrated here. The coronal plane is even with the midline of the body, and is what you see facing forward.

The sagital plane divides right and left, and the transverse plane divides the top half of your body from the bottom.

The convention is that movements are referenced from the anatomical position, shown left.

Hyper- can be added to any movement to denote movement beyond the normal range.

Anatomical Motions and Their Opposites.

Abduction – Abduction involves drawing a body part away from the sagital plane, or in the case of hands and feet, spreading the toes or	**Adduction** – Adduction involves bringing a body part towards the sagital plane.

97

fingers.	
Flexion – Flexion denotes decreasing the angle of a joint. When you sit, your knees are flexed.	**Extension** – Extension denotes increasing the angle of a joint. When you stand, your knees are extended.
Medial Rotation – Rotation towards the coronal plane, i.e., turning your arms or legs inwards.	**Lateral Rotation** – Rotation away from the coronal plane, i.e., turning your arms or legs outward.
Elevation – Moving a body part upwards. The first part of shrugging your shoulders.	**Depression**- Moving a body part downwards. The second part of shrugging your shoulders.

Motions that Involve just the Feet or Hands.

Supination – Moving the palm so that it faces up, i.e., holding a bowl of soup.	**Pronation** – Rotating the palm so that it faces down. I.e., pouring out a bowl of soup.
Plantarflexion- Flexing the foot downward, i.e. pushing down on the gas pedal or flexing for a roundhouse kick.	**Dorsiflexion** – Bringing the foot upwards, i.e. taking the foot off the gas pedal.
Inversion- Bringing the sole of the foot inwards, i.e., as during a side kick.	**Eversion**- Bringing the sole of the foot outwards.

All body motions can be described with a combination of the preceding motions. However, while it might be technically correct to tell a student *"When chambering a low block, pronate your blocking hand while supinating the other hand,"* that would probably cause more confusion than it would alleviate. So when could you use these terms?

Each motion has specific muscles and joints that activate it. When a student has an injury, you should first seek to understand what specific motion caused the injury. If the injury is more serious, this information will help the doctor.

When learning a new move, it is important to understand all of the movements. These terms will help to understand the different movements.

It is helpful to describe submissions or other joint locks in anatomical terms to be perfectly clear. For instance, an arm bar uses hyperextension of the elbow, while an ankle lock uses hyperplantarflexion of the ankle. Understanding the precise mechanics of submissions results in less wasted effort.

If you break each move down into its individual components, you can more easily determine where a student is going wrong. Work on just that one movement, and the overall technique will improve.

If you find common motions in several techniques, working only on those motions will improve several techniques. For example, hip and knee flexion (lifting knees) is a motion that is important in many kicks. That is why we practice lifting knees so much.

Lesson 29: Physiology of Training

It is important to understand the physiological effects of training on one's body, both on a general level and on an individual level in that everyone's body responds slightly differently to the types of training available. This section will briefly cover skeletal muscle and the cellular and molecular changes that happen during training.

Fatigue after an extensive workout is common. It can also happen even after a light workout if you are not consistently training. Fatigue is the decreased efficiency and capacity of work that can be done by a muscle or the person as a whole. There are two types of fatigue that will be mentioned here. The first is psychological fatigue, which is the most common type and usually the first that a person feels. Psychological fatigue is when a person perceives that any more work from the muscles is not possible. **This type of fatigue can be overcome!** Think of the last few seconds of a sparring match in a tournament. You are so tired that you can hardly bounce, but you are down by one point and then everybody starts to cheer you on and you feel yourself get excited and find the energy you didn't think that you had to throw one more fast kick to the head. That is an example of overcoming psychological fatigue.

The second type of fatigue is muscular fatigue, which is a physical fatigue that takes place in the muscle fibers. This is when there is too much ATP depletion in the muscle and muscle contraction can not function to full capacity. There is a physical decline in the tension that the muscle can produce. This fatigue is not perceived, but actual, and the muscles cannot be fully productive beyond this point. **Basically, this type of fatigue happens when your muscles have used up all the energy that they have, or have built up too many waste products to function efficiently.** The stronger and better conditioned you are, the more that you can delay this type of fatigue.

What causes sore muscles? After extensive training, when muscles feel sore for the next day or two, it is due to the fact that slight damage has occurred to the muscle and the surrounding connective tissue during a workout with repetitive moves that quickly contract the muscles, such as kicking drills or even lunges where the muscles are stretched before handling a load. The pain that you feel is inflammation from the muscles in response to the microtears in the muscles and connective tissue. Being slightly sore is not a bad thing. In fact it is the microtears that stimulate muscle growth. This is a healing process to build muscle, so it is not healthy to be training where you are sore every day. With consistent training your muscles should build to the point where you should not find yourself sore after most workouts, only those that are more extensive or active than usual, or those that focus on unique muscle groups that aren't used often.

Consistent exercise helps your muscles out in many more ways than just size and strength. There are two types of exercise: **aerobic, and anaerobic.** In martial arts, we use both types of exercise. We generally work from an aerobic base with anaerobic bursts. For instance, bouncing and moving around in a match is aerobic, but as soon as you go into a flurry and start kicking and kicking, your muscles are using oxygen faster than it can get to them, thus you are in an anaerobic state. This aerobic/anaerobic mix is one of the things that makes martial arts conditioning so difficult and unique. One good way to train is to go for a long jog, but alternate a minute or so of jogging with 15 seconds or so of sprinting. This will mix the two types of exercise in a way that you will need in the type of match you wish to compete in.

Aerobic Exercise - Aerobic exercise is when the body is working at a pace that oxygen delivery occurs at least as quickly as oxygen is being used in the cells for the production of energy. This is generally a decent cardio workout that is at a constant pace and doesn't leave you gasping for breath at the end of it. Aerobic exercise not only increases size, strength and endurance of muscles, it also increases the amount of nuclei, connective tissue, blood vessels and mitochondria that are associated with the muscles, increasing the potential overall performance of the muscles.

Anaerobic Exercise - Anaerobic exercise is basically when your body has used up your oxygenated energy, and now is producing the energy you need to continue through anaerobic respiration which is the production of energy in the absence of oxygen. This energy production is much more limited in duration than aerobic energy, but is a fast production of energy for sprinting or fast double kicks and has the metabolic byproduct of **lactic acid**. Lactic acid build up is responsible for the "knots" in your muscles, and is released from the muscle fibers into the blood stream. Lactic acid is also responsible for the soreness that you feel after a workout. Too much lactic acid in the blood stream can make you sick, so it is very good to drink a lot of water after any good workout and the day after to help move it through your system.

Muscle relaxation is the opposite of contraction, yet it also requires energy. Energy is required in the transportation of specific elements within the muscle cells, and once these elements bind to a specific site, if the muscles need to contract again, more energy is needed than if the muscle hadn't relaxed in the first place. This is just to illustrate that it is not energy efficient to let muscles relax in the middle of a long workout. It is best to let the muscles relax at the end of your use of them unless you plan to work out for half a day or more at one time. **The elements that are required are Calcium, Sodium, and Potassium. A lack of any of these can lead to difficulty contracting and relaxing muscles.** This is essentially what happens during a cramp. These elements are known as electrolytes, and are a major component of sports drinks.

Some people use anabolic steroids to increase the size and strength of their muscles. Anabolic steroids are similar to testosterone in that they increase the size of muscles. However, studies have shown many severe side effects with the use of anabolic steroids including heart attacks, strokes, testicular atrophy, irritability, sterility and abnormal liver function.

Lesson 30: Foot and Ankle

As martial artists, we use our feet a lot, and therefore have many common injuries in this part of our bodies. As instructors it is necessary to understand basic anatomy, common injuries, and how to properly treat injuries.

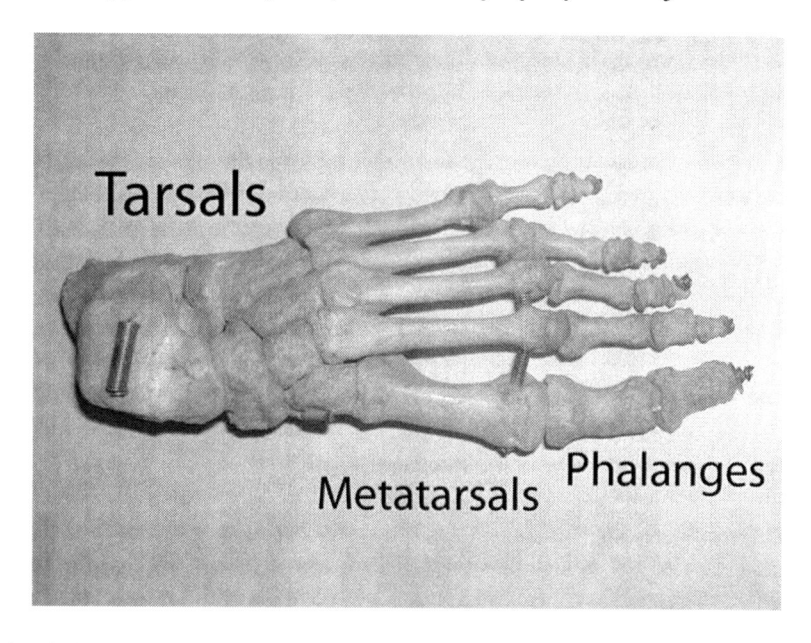

The basic bones of the foot and ankle for you to know are the **tarsal bones**, (ankle bones) which connect to the two lower leg bones – **tibia** and **fibula**. Sprains and twisted ankles occur in this region through the muscles, tendons and ligaments of the ankle.

The long bones in the foot which make up what we call the instep are the metatarsal bones. This area gets bruised often from kicking elbows, and the bones can break from landing incorrectly.

The toe bones are called **phalanges**, and will sometimes get sprained or broken. This happens from running when a toe catches on the mat or a target is kicked improperly.

One of the most common ankle injuries is a **sprain**. Once an ankle has been sprained badly, it will be much more vulnerable to further sprains in the future. Therefore, you may have many students who come in and have already suffered these sprains in the past. They are usually used to the injuries but they will still hurt. Ankle braces can be helpful for such cases.

For any minor sprains or strains of the ankle or toes, the injuries must be wrapped properly with athletic tape or an ace bandage before walking, running or training on it. To wrap, begin above where there is pain, and wrap beyond the injury and then back to the beginning for support. It is important to wrap tight enough for support, but do not cut off circulation or cause major discomfort. Sometimes, when a person breaks a toe, they might be worried, especially if they have never broken a bone before. However, there is not much that even a doctor can do for a broken toe. The toe should be 'buddy taped' to the one next to it. Have the student avoid contact with that foot, but otherwise they should be able to train normally.

Plantar fasciitis is a strain on the ligament that runs from the heel of the foot to the ball. The strain causes localized pain in the heel and arch of the foot and is caused by increased activity and is associated with age. Localized stretching and icing of the area is a common treatment. To train with **plantar fasciitis**, the arch of the foot must be taped well to maintain the arch while reliving tension from the plantar fascia. (Taekwondo shoes would be recommended in addition.)

Achilles Tendon Bursitis is a common foot pain in athletes. The bursa, a small sac of fluid between the tendon and bone, becomes inflamed with repeated trauma. This causes pain at the back of the heel along with swelling and tenderness. If fingers are pressed on either side of the heel, a spongy resistance may be felt. The conservative treatments for this are anti-inflammatories, icing, and rest.

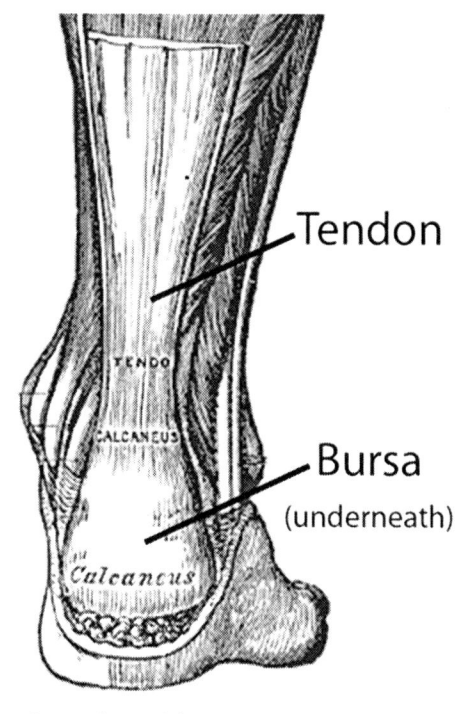

Achilles Tendonitis is a more common injury for runners or high heel wearers than martial artists but it can happen to your students too. The **Achilles tendon** is the large tendon that connects at the heel and the two large calf muscles. This tendon gets strained or can be torn or snapped by being over-elongated. Overuse, and doing too much too soon, running uphill or on the balls of your feet can put too much tension on the tendon and cause inflammation, tenderness, pain, redness and more. The **Achilles tendon** has poor blood supply and is very slow to heal. Anti-inflammatories, ice, rest and taping the back of the heel and leg can help relieve symptoms.

Athlete's foot (Tenea pedis) is a fungal infection on the skin of the feet, usually starting between the toes, and may be transmitted from infected humans, animals or soil. The symptoms include: itching, scaling, flaking, blisters and cracked skin. Broken skin can lead to secondary bacterial infections in addition to the fungal infections and then antibiotics must be taken. For just the fungal infection there are many over the counter and prescription medications for treatment. It is important to recognize and treat athlete's foot as quickly as possible to prevent spreading it to other people in the school since we are bare footed most of the time. Good hygiene is key to avoiding athlete's foot. The fungus thrives in moist areas, so keeping gear and shoes clean and dry is very important.

Lesson 31: Shin and Knee

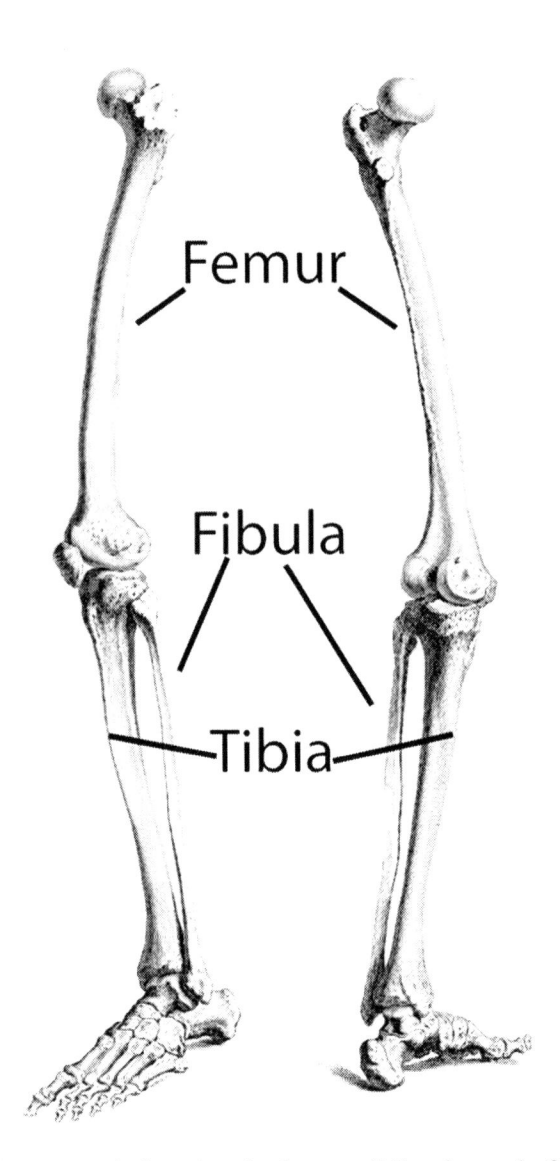

The knee is one of the most important joints for Martial artists. Not only is it important for kicking, its function is critical for running, generating power for jumping and cushioning impacts from landing. Because of this, the knee is one of the most frequently injured joints, especially as the age or weight of the student increases.

Anatomy

The knee is comprised of all four leg bones: the **femur** which is the thigh bone, a long and thick bone which is very hard to break. The two lower leg bones are the **tibia**, which is the large shin bone, and the **fibula**, which is the smaller lower leg bone and is important for muscle attachment and rotation. The last bone is the **patella**, which is known as the knee cap. The knee has two types of cartilage: **articular** and **meniscal**. Both types of cartilage are important in keeping the bones gliding instead of grinding against each other and distributing weight correctly.

Stabilizing the knee joint are four ligaments: The **lateral collateral ligament (LCL)** located on the "outside" of the knee, the **medial collateral ligament (MCL)** located on the "inside" of the knee, the **anterior cruciate ligament (ACL)** located in the front, and the **posterior cruciate ligament (PCL)** is in the back. The ACL and PCL cross paths, hence — cruciate.

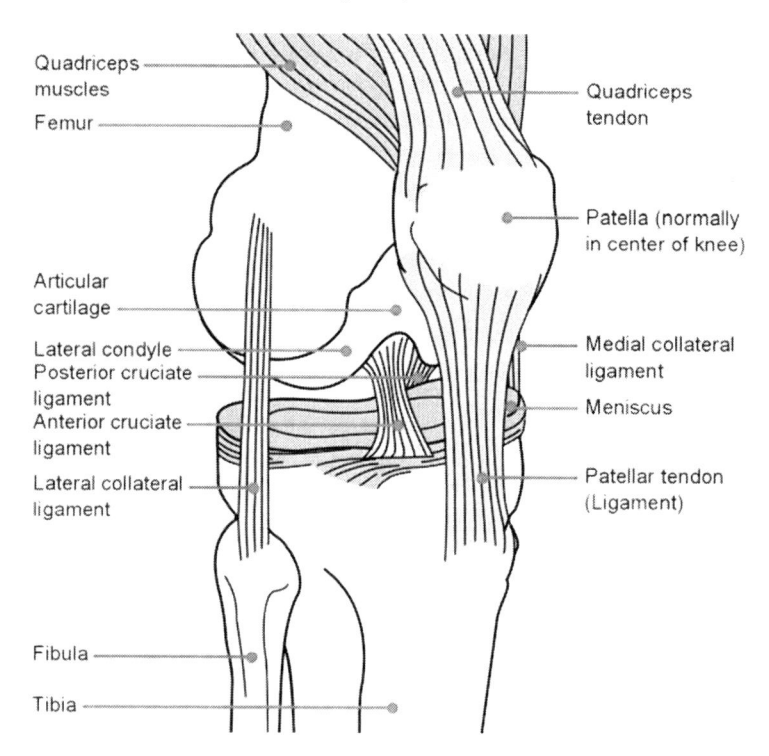

```
Quadriceps muscles
Femur
Quadriceps tendon
Patella (normally in center of knee)
Articular cartilage
Lateral condyle
Posterior cruciate ligament
Anterior cruciate ligament
Medial collateral ligament
Meniscus
Patellar tendon (Ligament)
Lateral collateral ligament
Fibula
Tibia
```

Common Injuries

Note: Because of poor blood supply of ligaments and their importance to motion, torn ligaments often require surgery before students will be able to engage in martial arts again. As always, a physician will make the official diagnosis.

Meniscal Tear – The meniscus is a tough cartilaginous disc that distributes weight between the **femur** and the **tibia**. There are two menisci in each knee, a lateral and a medial. Tears in the menisci occur sometimes in athletes when there is severe trauma to the knee, or if the knee is bent and then twisted or rotated. Symptoms include: knee pain, (sometimes very acute) swelling, clicking, popping or limited motion of the knee. This injury is often times accompanied by injuries to one or more or the knee ligaments. Treatment is usually long and annoying because the meniscus is cartilage and has limited blood supply and is therefore slow to heal. During the healing process, the torn cartilage interferes with clean movement of the knee and can lead to long and painful rehabilitation where the person should not engage in most martial arts activities. Some tears are too severe and require orthopedic surgery to cut and clear away damaged cartilage for the knee to function properly.

Knee Hyperextension – Hyperextension means over extending/straightening, or bending backwards. Care should be taken when students kick the air, especially when snapping during forms, or else they may hyperextend the knee. This is generally not a problem unless students strongly kick the air a lot. It can usually be solved by rest and icing the affected area.

ACL Tear – This happens with excessive rotation. The knee suddenly gives way, and there may be a 'pop' sound. There will be pain and swelling in the knee. This will usually require surgery to fix as well.

PCL Tear – This happens when the tibia is forced backwards. The symptoms are similar to those of an ACL tear.

MCL Tear – This happens when the outside of the knee is struck, and often the knee buckles. Symptoms include swelling, bruising, joint pain and instability in the knee.

Shin Splints – Shin splints is a broad term to describe general shin pain. The most common cause is small tears in the muscles where they attach to the shin bones. This happens from overuse, jumping, or running, and can be slow to heal. The best remedy is sufficient rest. Ice, anti-inflammatory, and acupuncture can also help. A proper diet and a healthy intake of calcium and protein have been proven to help heal and prevent shin splints.

Shin Bruises – Bruises to the shin are very common in sparring. Treat them like any other bruises.

Shin Conditioning – Muy Thai is famous for shin conditioning. In fact, athletes in Thailand will even kick trees to deaden nerves and make their bone denser. However, this is only done with a certain, specific type of spongy tree. Also, this is only done after the shins are already conditioned. Sometimes, other martial arts athletes will hear about this and go off kicking trees or putting rolling pins down their shins, causing themselves much harm and little good. To gradually and correctly condition shins, students should spend much time kicking heavy bags of gradually increasing hardness, however, nothing harder than packed rice. Shins will naturally condition over time, especially with sparring practice.

Duck walks and Frog Jumps – These can be very helpful in strengthening of students, yet can also injure the knee. The best rule of thumb is to use them, but sparingly, in children and healthy younger adults, and not at all in older adults, overweight students, and students with a history of knee problems. Also, plyometrics should be used only sparingly in students who are overweight or who have knee problems.

Lesson 32: Hip

The hip joint is formed from the head of the **femur** and the **acetabulum** of the pelvis in a **ball and socket joint.** Both surfaces are covered in cartilage to cushion the joint. The hip joint has five ligaments, but tearing these is rare because of the strength of the joint and the muscles around it. Any injury that has enough force to tear the hip joint would be a very serious injury. This is also why there are very few grappling submissions that attack the hip joints.

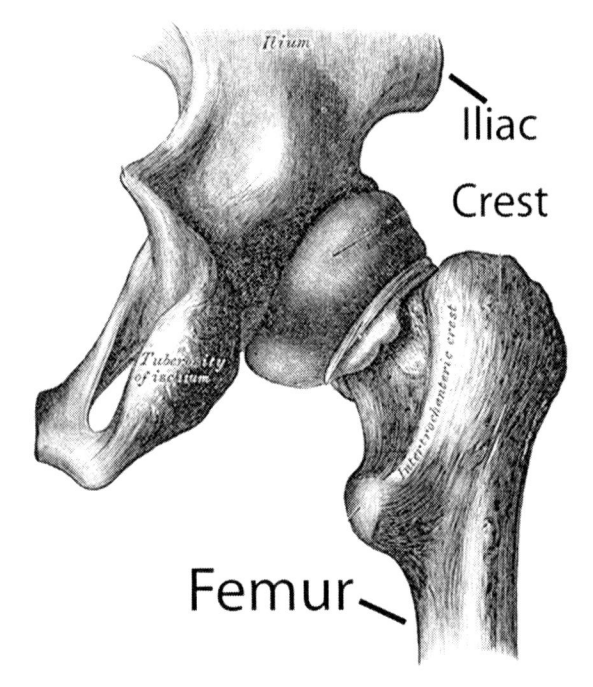

Hip joints are different in males and females to facilitate childbirth. In general, females have wider hips to make an opening for the birth canal. This can make some techniques such as double kicks more difficult for some women to accomplish.

Hips are critically important for all kicking techniques. Make sure that the hips are well warmed up with exercises that naturally increase the range of motion of the joint.

Hip Fracture – Hip fractures are more common in older students, or in people who are no longer training. Hip fractures can result from **osteoporosis** (where bones have become porous through years,) **osteonecrosis** (where bones die due to lack of sufficient blood flow,) and through trauma caused by a fall. A hip fracture is a very debilitating injury, since the hip joint is required for walking or even crawling.

Osteoporosis is a condition that will usually only affect older people, but studies have shown that exercise such as martial arts training done throughout life can increase bone density and protect against osteoporosis later on.

Lesson 33: Core

Ribs - Humans have 12 pairs of ribs, each connecting to one of the 12 **thoracic vertebrae**. The first 10 wrap around and connect to **costal cartilage** forming a protective "cage" around many of our vital organs. The last two pair are known as **floating ribs**.

Broken ribs occur with chest trauma and can happen with a really hard kick. Symptoms of a broken rib include general pain of the area, and acute pain when being pressed on or breathing in.

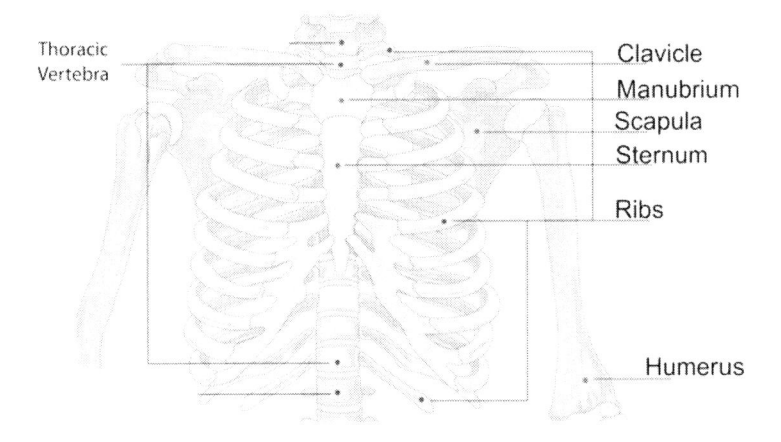

In most cases there is little that doctors can do to help fix a broken rib; generally pain killers, wrapping and rest for one to two months is what it takes. The real danger with breaking a rib is the broken rib puncturing one of the organs that it usually protects, which is why going to the doctor after any injury that might have broken a rib is recommended.

Another injury that can happen is a tearing of the **intercostal cartilage**. This is painful, and can cause the ribs to pop out of place. This can happen with torsion of the body, as in grappling.

The Spleen - The spleen is one of the largest organs in the body and serves as part of the blood production and filtering system. It is located under the left side of the rib cage and can be injured with direct contact to that area. The spleen acts as a reservoir of red blood cells and is a producer of white blood cells; therefore, an injury to it can result in blood spilling into the abdomen. However, the organ is encased in a tough, fibrous capsule that helps hold it in place.

When an athlete has mononucleosis, "mono" or the "kissing disease" they are strongly encouraged not to participate in any contact sports, (including sparring and grappling,) because the spleen is very active in producing antibodies for the immune system and enlarges to produce more white blood cells. The enlarged spleen will often protrude lower than the ribs and is at risk of rupturing with a direct blow to the left side.

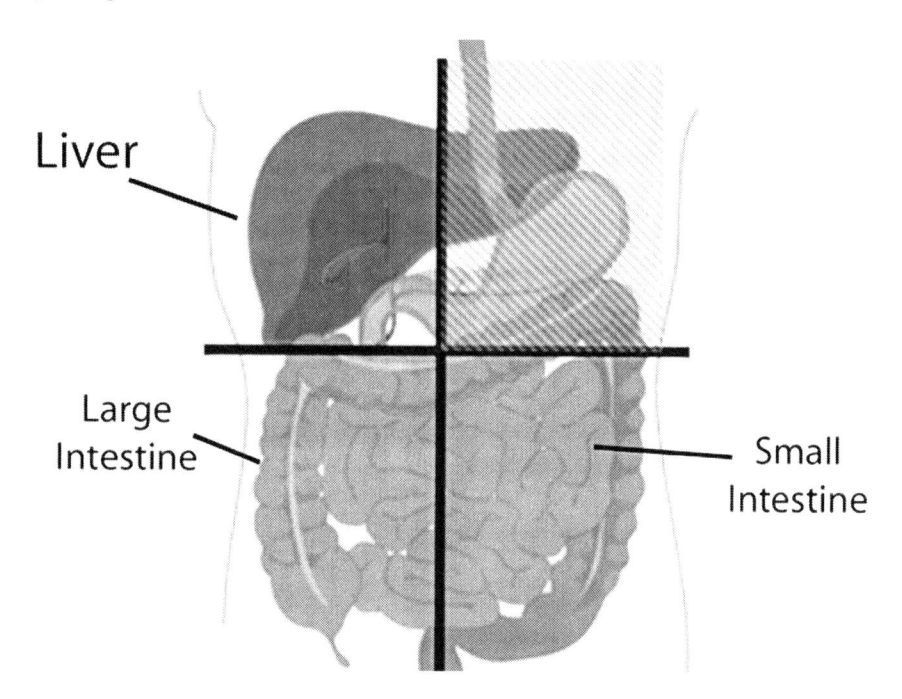

The Liver – The liver is an organ that plays a major role in storage, metabolism, protein synthesis and detoxification. Liver lacerations or injury during sports is very rare, and if any injury seems like it has damaged any organs, the person should be taken to the nearest emergency room.

The Kidneys – The kidneys (usually two) are located just under the ribs in the middle of the back. They function in removing toxins, regulating water within the body, controlling chemicals and regulating hormones. Though the kidneys are well protected by back muscles and ribs, getting kicked in the back can possibly, though rarely, break ribs and/or cause blunt trauma to the kidneys. Signs of kidney injury are flank pain, broken ribs in the back, blood in urine, and shock. Sparrers are recommended to get a hogu with back protection. When a person's kidney fails, then they must use a dialysis machine. The dialysis machine is basically an artificial kidney that takes a person's blood and filters it, returning it to the bloodstream.

In general, internal injuries must be taken seriously. As martial artists, we take shots to the body all the time. How do we know when to suspect an internal injury? **Here are some signs:**

- **Something just doesn't feel right** – Most martial artists know what it feels like to get kicked. If something feels abnormal, this is a sign there may be a problem.

- **Blood in the urine or stool.** – This is a bad sign, as something inside has broken.

- **Deep, discolored bruises** – May be a sign of serious internal bleeding

- **Any signs of shock** – Again, may be a sign of bleeding or abnormal organ function.

What can we do to prevent core injuries?

- **Strenghen Bodies** – Having stronger stomach and back muscles and overall physical strength will go a long way.

- **Wear proper protection** – Including feet pads and wrap around hogus.

- **Ensure control in student mismatches** – Never partner strong students who lack control with significantly smaller ones.

Lesson 34: Spine

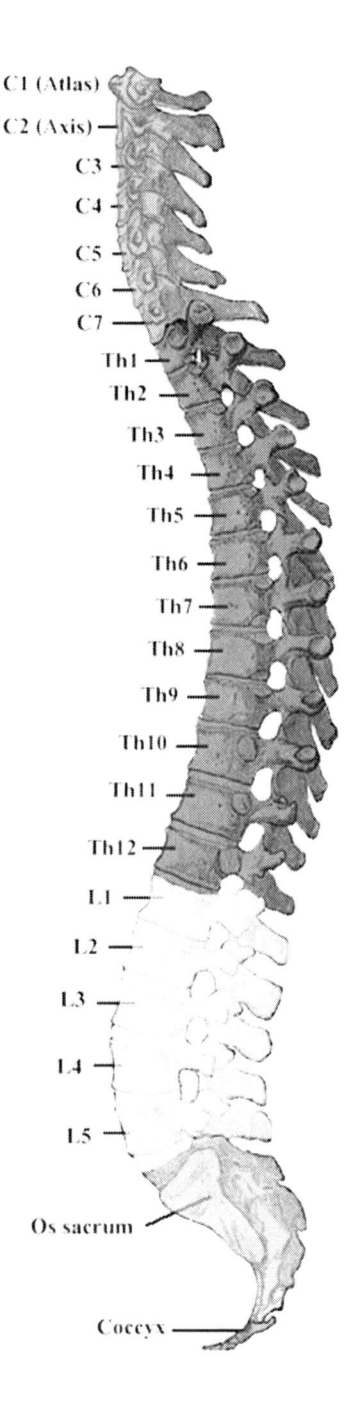

Although all areas of the body are critical, the spine and brain are probably the most important because they coordinate the rest of the body's function. Because of this, there are generally no manipulations of the spine allowed in free grappling. Although we may teach how to counter these moves, students should use them only in an emergency. The spine has 33 bones which are divided into the **Cervical** (neck), **Thoracic** (chest), **Lumbar** (lower back), **Sacrum**, and **Cocyx** (tailbone). The spine houses the spinal cord, a bundle of nerves that gives and receives signals from the rest of the body. The exception to this is 12 **cranial nerves**, which innervate several structures directly from the brain. The following diagram shows the bones.

Spinal Fracture – A spinal fracture is a break in any part of the spine. This break could be along the edge, or could cut through the spinal cord. Fractures cutting through the spinal cord could cause paralysis.

Herniated disk – When the disks that cushion the spinal cord segments break open due to disease, injury, or overuse, they can push on the nerve root and cause pain. This can also cause difficulty of movement, due to the fact that the vertebra is now no longer properly cushioned.

Normal Vertebra (Top View)

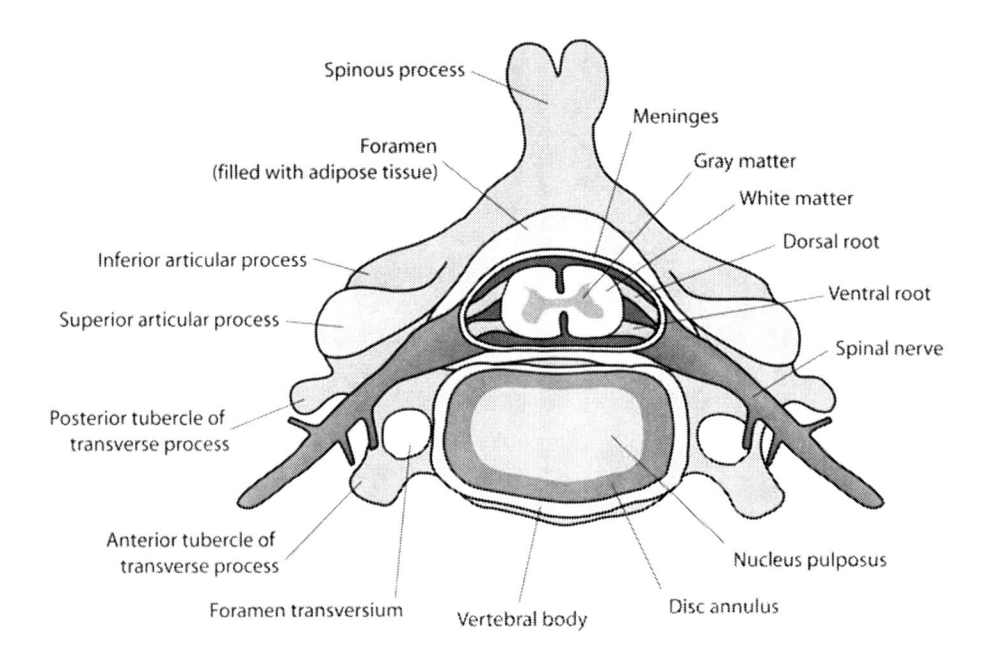

Herniated Disk (Top View)

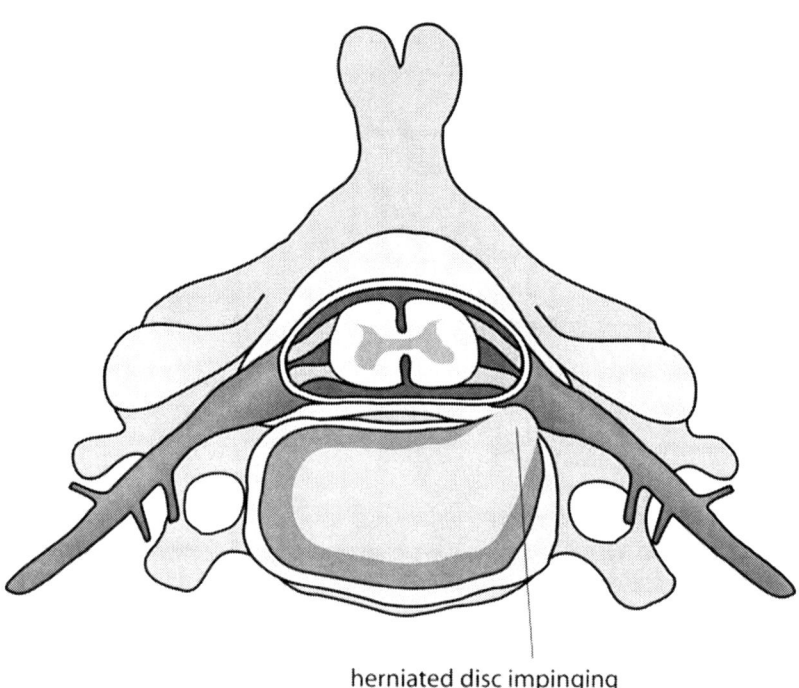

herniated disc impinging
on spinal nerve

First aid – If you ever suspect a spinal injury, **DO NOT MOVE THE PERSON!** It is possible to make things much worse by moving them. The only exception would be a truly life threatening situation, such as the immediate need to begin CPR. Call 911 so that the EMTs can bring the patient to the hospital where the doctors can take an x-ray before attempting treatment.

Pinched nerve – A pinched nerve happens when a muscle, bone, swelling, herniated disk, etc. presses on a nerve. It can cause pain, tingling, or even rarely a loss of function. Pinched nerves can usually be fixed with rest, but may sometimes require surgery.

Lesson 35: Shoulder

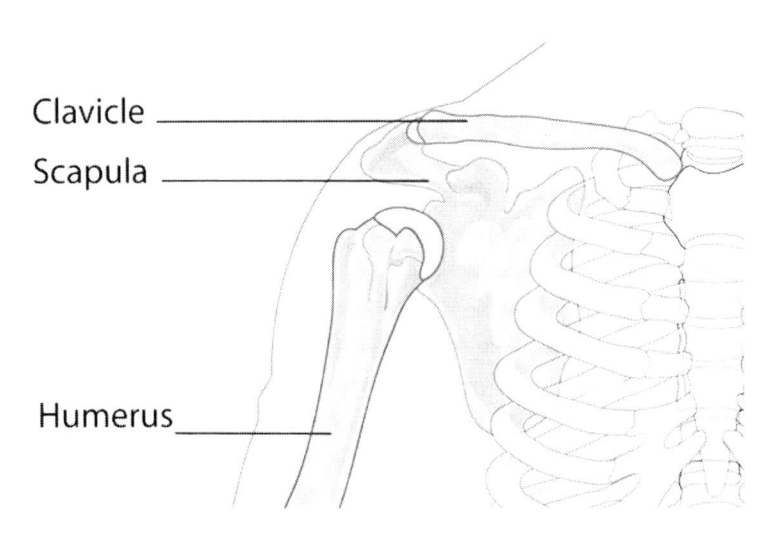

Clavicle
Scapula
Humerus

The shoulder joint is the most flexible joint in the human body. What we usually refer to as the shoulder is actually the **glenohumeral joint**. The shoulder joint is made up of three bones, the **clavicle**, the **humerus**, and the **scapula**.

Because the shoulder has such a wide range of motion, it is also more vulnerable to problems than the hip, the other main ball and socket joint.

Rotator Cuff - The rotator cuff is comprised of the muscles and tendons that hold the ball of the **humerus** tight into the shoulder joint. Any of these muscles or tendons can be torn when too much force is applied, especially in a circular manner (i.e., baseball pitchers). If the rotator cuff becomes inflamed, standard **P.R.I.C.E.** (Pause, Rest, Ice, Compression, Elevation) may be used to heal it. Physical therapy exercises may also strengthen it. However, if the rotator cuff becomes fully torn, surgery is usually required. Torn rotator cuff injuries are rare in martial arts, partly because the variety of pushups we do can act to strengthen the rotator cuff.

Dislocation - Dislocation occurs when the humerus slips out of its socket. This can often be sudden and extremely painful. The treatment is to pop the shoulder back into place; however, as we are not doctors, we should not attempt to pop it back. However, you can help the student to do it themselves, especially if they have had dislocations before. The pain will usually subside when the shoulder is popped back into place. If someone has an easily dislocated shoulder, consider not allowing grappling submissions that partly or completely attack the shoulder, such as kimura locks and bent and straight arm bars.

Inflammation - Inflammation can be a problem, especially in older students. This can happen when the bursa that cushions the shoulder dry out or when the cartilage wears down. In this case, ice can be helpful. The student might have to do less pushups or hard punching and blocking motions.

Lesson 36: Hand and Arm

The arm has one upper/**proximal** (close to the body core) long bone – the **humerus**, and two lower/**distal** (away from the body) long bones – the **radius** and **ulna**. The arm also has the wrist, hand and finger bones – **carpals, metacarpals** and **phalanges** respectively.

Overall the arm has amazing rotation. In the upper arm, this is due to the shoulder joint mentioned previously. The lower arm rotation is due to three joints at the elbow which allow for general flexion and extension of the arm, and also rotation of the radius around the ulna.

To elaborate on the anatomical motions mentioned earlier, when your hands are at your side, open and palms are facing forward, or elbow is **flexed** (bent) and palms are facing up – the ulna and radius are now parallel to each other this is called **supination**. (Hint to help remember this – think of holding a bowl of soup, palms up or out – supinated.) When rotated from this position – the palm facing down or back, the radius has now rotated around the stationary ulna and has taken the hand with it – the radius is now crossed over the ulna and the hand is now **pronated**. (Think of this as pouring out the soup.)

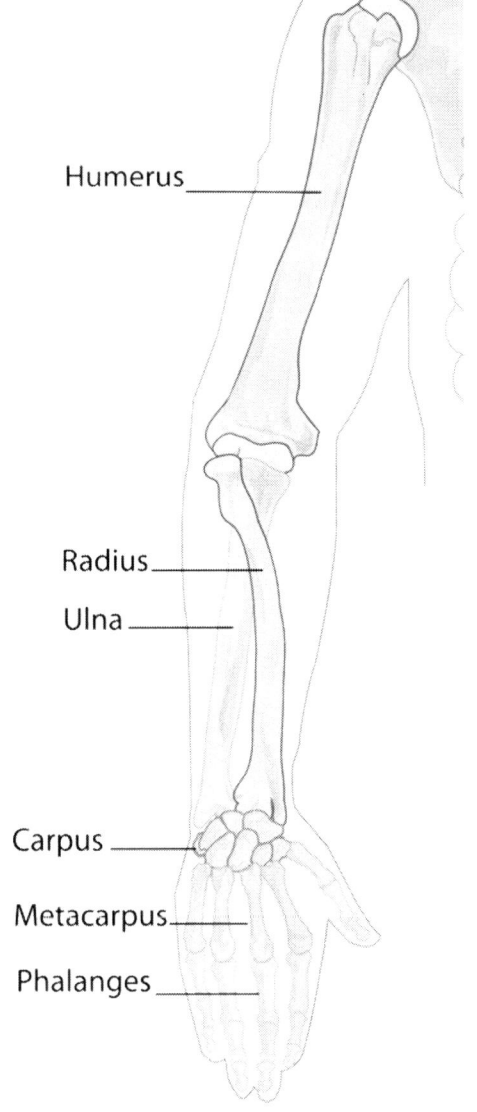

The ulna makes up most of the elbow joint with the humerus, whereas the radius makes up most of the wrist joint with the carpals. Any long bone injury at the elbow will generally involve the ulna, whereas any long bone injury in the wrist is likely to involve the radius which is attached at the thumb side of the hand. The bones classified as long bones are the humerus, radius and ulna in the arm. The only other long bones in the human body are in the legs and are the femur, tibia and fibula.

Injuries and conditions

For martial artists, these injuries may occur during sparring when a kick catches a finger or is sometimes powerful enough to break one of the long bones in the arm that was used to block. Incorrect falling technique can yield fractured wrists and elbows and strain tendons or muscles on the shoulder.

General **bruising, sprains** and **strains** happen with any sport and can generally be treated at home with ice and rest.

For **fractures** and **dislocations**, the general symptoms include:
- Severe pain, general swelling in the area, joint is bent at an odd angle, joint locked or has abnormal movement, numbness or tingling.

- Some people may have common joint dislocations and know how to put it back into place and might ask for help. The joint will usually need to be pulled beyond where it normally sits before it settles back into place. Any dislocation can cause tendon, ligament, blood vessel or muscle damage and should generally be seen by a physician. If you attempt to help someone pull a dislocated joint back into place and they scream, struggle a great deal or pass out – stop immediately and get them into a doctor or E.R. as something is probably broken or abnormally twisted or torn. **Note: Putting dislocations into place should only be done by a doctor or by the person themselves if they have done it before**.

Any possible fractures to the long bones should be treated immediately by a doctor.

Nursemaid's Elbow – Nursemaid's Elbow is a dislocation of the elbow, and is fairly common in 1-3 year olds. This happens when the child is falling and an adult holding the hand does not let go, or by trying to pull a child up by the arm, or any tugging motion. The connection of the tendon is not very well developed until four or five. The child will generally have some initial pain, though not always severe, and will not want to use the afflicted arm or be able to raise it above the elbow. Once the arm is rotated back into place, the child will have full use of the arm within 30 minutes. A child who has a previous history of Nursemaid's elbow is more susceptible to it until they are 5 years old. When working with Little Tigers, always lift or catch by the body or under the arm pits.

Overuse injuries

Osteoarthritis - Osteoarthritis is the most common form of **arthritis**. The symptoms include: reduced motion in joints, swelling and pain. It can occur in any joint, but usually it affects your hands, knees, hips or spine. **Cartilage** is the slippery tissue that covers the ends of bones in a joint and absorbs the shock of movement; osteoarthritis breaks down that cartilage. When you lose cartilage, your bones rub together and over time, this rubbing can permanently damage the joint. Factors that may cause osteoarthritis include: joint injury, being overweight, or getting older.

Carpal Tunnel Syndrome (CTS) - CTS presents with pressure on the nerve of the wrist. Symptoms include numbness of the wrist, fingers and sometimes arm, a tingling sensation, weakness and pain of the hand and wrist when in use. CTS is a symptom, not a disease and can be caused by overuse or an underlying disease. Rest, ice, anti-inflammatory, and perhaps a change in overuse such as a wrist rest on a key board can help.

Tendinosis and Tendonitis - **Tendonosis** is caused by small tears (microtears) in the tissues around the tendon causing tendon pain. **Tendinitis** is inflammation around the tendon and usually occurs in conjunction with tendinosis. Any activity that requires rapid joint movements or repeated twisting, such as certain sports (martial arts) or jobs, can cause a tendon injury. Aging can also be a factor, as the wear and tear that occurs to tendons over time can also make them vulnerable to injury. Common symptoms of tendon injury include pain, tenderness, and decreased strength and movement in the affected area.

Lesson 37: The Eye

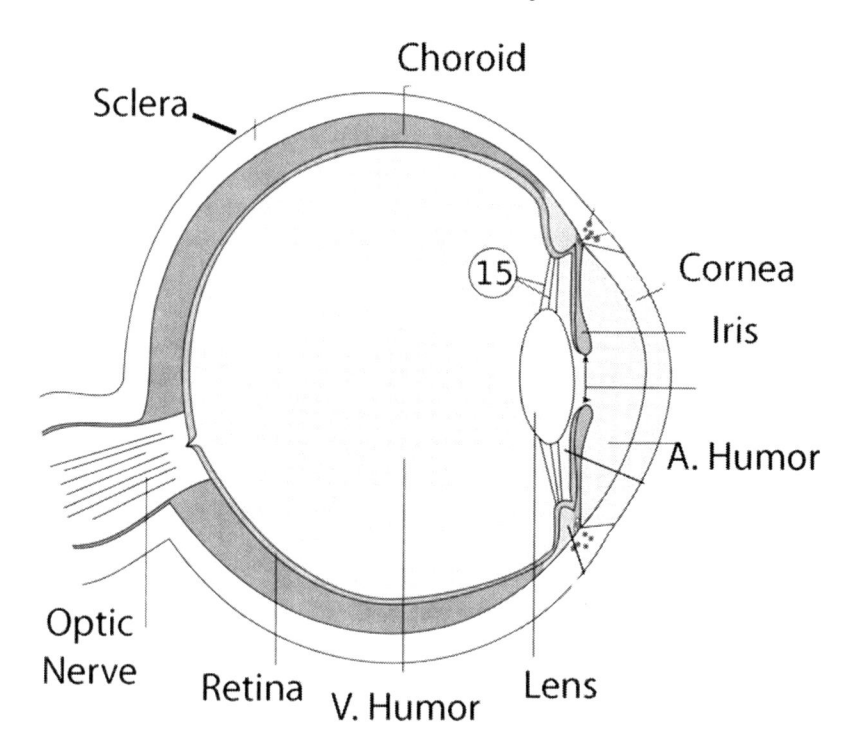

Diagram labels: Choroid, Sclera, 15, Cornea, Iris, A. Humor, Optic Nerve, Retina, V. Humor, Lens

The eye is the key organ for sight in humans. When the eyelid is open, light comes in through the **cornea** and **lens**, which together focus light on the **macula lutea**, the center of the Rods and Cones. The Rods see black and white light, while the three types of cones, Red, Green, and Blue, see those colors. These cones have pigments in them that are activated when certain wavelengths of light (colors) strike their surfaces. This activity results in firings along the **optic nerve** which leads the brain to interpret the vision.

The shape of the eye is determined by the **vitreous humor** (gel-like substance inside the eye) and the muscles that can change the shape slightly so that the image hits the **macula lutea** exactly. This is called focusing, and the eye will change shape, depending on how far away the object that the eye is focusing on is. The **macula lutea** is the part of the **retina** where most of the rods and cones are concentrated. Often, there is some problem with the cornea or lens and the eye cannot focus the image directly on the macula. This causes the image to be slightly blurry. This can be fixed by glasses or contacts, which bend the light entering them to compensate and put the image back on the macula.

A surgery that has become common recently is radial keratotomy. This is where a doctor will use a laser to cut several slits along the radius of the cornea. These slits will cause the cornea to contract and settle into a new shape. This can save the patient from ever having to wear glasses or contacts again.

The Pupil - The pupil dilates (gets bigger) or constricts (gets smaller) to allow more or less light to enter the eye. This serves the same function as the ear muscles that dampen the incus, malleus, and stapes. This is also why when you get up at night to go to the bathroom and turn on the light, your eye will hurt. An old "ninja legend" is that you can tell time by looking in a cat's eye, although, looking at the position of the sun is probably easier and more accurate.

Depth Perception - Just as in the ear, having two eyes is important for depth perception. This allows us to see how far things are from us, or live in 3D. Without this, everything would look like a picture, where every object in the picture is the same distance away. Some types of eye conditions can cause this. Obviously, depth perception is critical in sparring.

Colorblindness - Colorblindness occurs when one of the types of cones doesn't function correctly. The most common type is the loss of red vision in males. A simple test can tell if you can see red or not. Most people will see a number, people who cannot see red will see nothing at all. Interestingly, colorblindness does have some advantages. Colorblind people initially see better in the dark and are also able to see through camouflage more easily than people will all their rods functioning correctly.

The test image will not work in a black and white book, thus the original image has been placed at www.kattaekwondo.com/colortest.jpg

Common Injuries and Treatment

Perhaps the most common injury is getting debris in the eye. This could include sand, sweat, eyelashes, etc. The treatment is to flush the affected area with water, and further attention is usually not required. If large debris is lodged in the eye (i.e., stick, knife, etc.), do not attempt to remove it. Instead, stabilize the debris and seek immediate medical attention.

Unfortunately, eye injuries from blunt trauma could present a danger in Taekwondo or other contact martial arts. However, international regulations state that no eye protection is to be worn. We do offer some protection by wearing pads on the striking surfaces. For students at elevated risk of eye injury, consider the following: no sparring, no head contact sparring, or sparring with a face shield. Certain manufacturers do make face shields for sparring, although they are not generally worn as they present their own issues. Sports are the number one cause of eye injuries in the United States.

Peripheral Vision - This refers to seeing something in the periphery, or just outside of the main area of focus. Objects in the periphery will be poorly defined, but you will notice just their presence or motion. Although it is hard to expand this, you can start to pay more attention to it, as it is critical when facing multiple opponents. 2 on 1 and 3 on 1 sparring are great for training this quality.

Eyes as Signals - It's often said that the eye is the mirror of the soul. Looking into someone's eye is a great way to help see what they are really thinking. Also, after a hard head contact, check a student's pupils. If they are dilated (bigger than normal) this is a sign of a concussion. If one is much bigger than the other, or if the eyes are unfocused and moving out of sync, this is a more serious sign. Looking for these signs is critical because any student with a concussion should not spar again for 30 days.

Lesson 38: The Ear

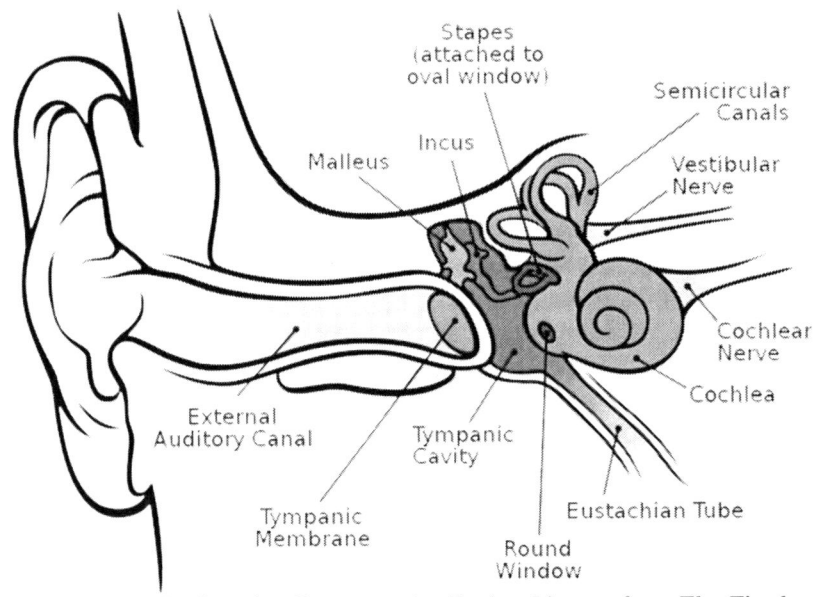

Image used under the Creative Commons Attribution License from <u>The Final Frontier, A PLoS Biology Vol. 3, No. 4, e137 doi:10.1371/journal.pbio.0030137</u>

The ear is a very important organ in the body that has two key functions. The first, of course, is hearing. The ear transfers sound wave energy into nerve impulse energy. First, the outer ear catches and slightly amplifies the sound as it narrows. The eardrum acts like a drum that causes the **malleus**, **incus**, and **stapes** bones to vibrate along the same patters. The stapes pushes on fluid in the **cochlea**, which transfers these fluctuating fluds waves to waves of tiny hairs in the **organ of corti**. The signals travel along the **vestibular cochlear nerve** and to the brain where they are processed. The second function of the ear is balance.

A defect in the eardrum or three inner ear bones is serious, but can be overcome by something called a **cochlear implant**. This is a microphone that connects directly to the cochlea and transfers the sound it hears to pulses which can be understood by the wearer's brain.

Decibel level - Sound is measured in decibels. The key thing to remember about the decibel level is that it is a logarithmic scale. Thus, 20 decibels is twice as loud as 10, and 30 decibels is 4 times (not 3) as loud as 10. 40 decibels is 8 times as loud as 10. Every time the decibel level increases by 10, the sound intensity doubles. Here are some decibel levels for common sounds.

Weakest sound heard	0 dB
Whisper Quiet Library	30 dB
Normal conversation (3-5')	60-70 dB
Truck Traffic	90 dB
Loud Rock Concert	115 dB
Pain	125 dB
Loudest recommended exposure (with protection) and gun blast	140 dB

It is important to note that there are generally three things that determine how much hearing damage there is— the intensity of the sound, the duration of the sound, and the background noise. The last one is interesting, and can be seen in cases of Eskimos with hearing loss. There was a famous study that found many Eskimos going deaf from their hunting guns, while the same didn't happen to soldiers or people who were witnesses to shootings. The reason is that when the background noise is loud or at least prevalent, muscles in your middle ear clamp down on the three bones to cause them to vibrate less for a given decibel level, thus muffling the sound. They do this so that the sound waves aren't so strong that they damage the ear. So what happened to the Eskimos? Alone in the frozen tundra, their ears were fine tuned to pick up the most minute sounds. When they shot their guns, their ears were not damped at all, causing damage. By the way, ears aren't the only things that sound can damage. If you happen to be near a really loud sound (over 200 dB), you could be in trouble. For instance, people on a nearby island when the volcano Krakatoa exploded were killed when the sound waves hit their chests. Other people 3000 miles away heard the explosion.

Sound Localization: So what benefit does having two ears have, and why are they on the opposite sides of our head? The answer has to do with figuring out where a sound is coming from. As you can see from the drawing below (The large circle is a head with two ears, the small circle is the location of the sound, and the lines are the path the sound takes to get to the ear) if we know trigonometry, and the different times the signal gets to the brain, we can calculate where the sound came from. That's exactly the calculation your brain does. This is a critical skill when facing multiple opponents.

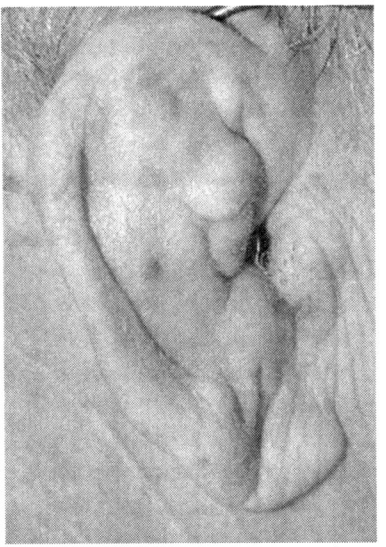

Cauliflower Ear – Cauliflower ear is a common ailment in wrestlers and grapplers, and can be prevented by simply wearing special grappling headgear. Basically, the cartilage separates from the perichrondium after a blow or other trauma to the ear. This causes a bruise to form. At this point, a doctor can treat the injury. However, when the injury is left and never treated, a permanent scarring can form.

It's generally not necessary to wear head protection for grappling intermittently, but serious grapplers should invest in ear protection. Cauliflower ear can also occur from sparring, but helmets should always be worn in Taekwondo sparring.

Ears and Balance: You might have noticed that the semicircular canals in the ear anatomy diagram in the beginning of this lesson look like the XYZ 3 dimensional graph axes, and you'd be absolutely correct. These fluid-filled canals also have hair cells that detect the movement of the fluid. Because of their shape, they can detect angular rotation in all 3 dimensions. The **sacculus** and the **uticle** are in the middle, and they detect movement in a straight line, for instance going forward or stopping. Balance is critically important in martial arts. Problems in these areas can cause a student to lose balance. By training, we learn to compensate for any errors our body makes and we also learn to understand the signals from these organs better. Be wary of kicks to the head, aside from causing concussions, they can also cause temporary loss of balance. As students get older, these hair cells die. So, just as older people lose their ability to hear, they also lose the ability to balance at a similar rate.

Lesson 39: Nervous System

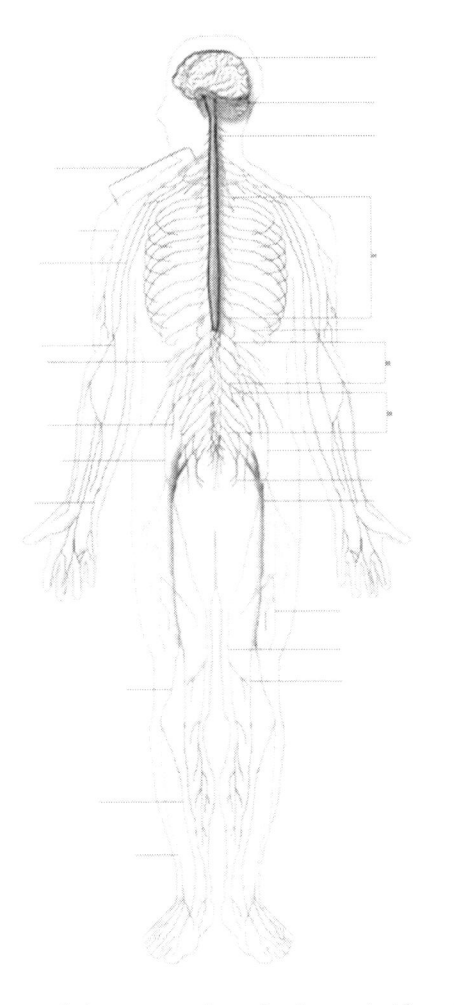

The nervous system is an incredibly important part of your body which helps you to be aware of your surroundings and respond to them. The main cells responsible for transmitting signals are called **neurons**. These cells are long cells that transmit information along their length via **electrical signals**.

At the end of each neuron, the electrical signal is converted to a chemical signal, which goes to the next neuron. **Sensory neurons** bring information to the brain, while **motor neurons** bring information from the brain to the muscles.

Incredibly complex networks of nerves are formed in the brain and spinal cord. One of the great remaining mysteries of science is if, and how, such networks could give rise to consciousness or the illusion of consciousness. Each of the nearly 100 billion neurons in the brain is connected to up to 1000 others, and has 1000 others connecting to it. If the majority of a cell's inputs fire, then that cell will fire as well.

The body of the neuron (**axon**) is covered by a **myelin sheath**. This increases the conduction speed because the electrical signals jump over the sheath and then re-fire. The exact physiology of this is interesting, but beyond this book. However, it is interesting to consider that the amount of myelenation of each neuron can affect the speed of that neuron. Faster nerve cells give a faster reaction time. They also give rise to the gate theory.

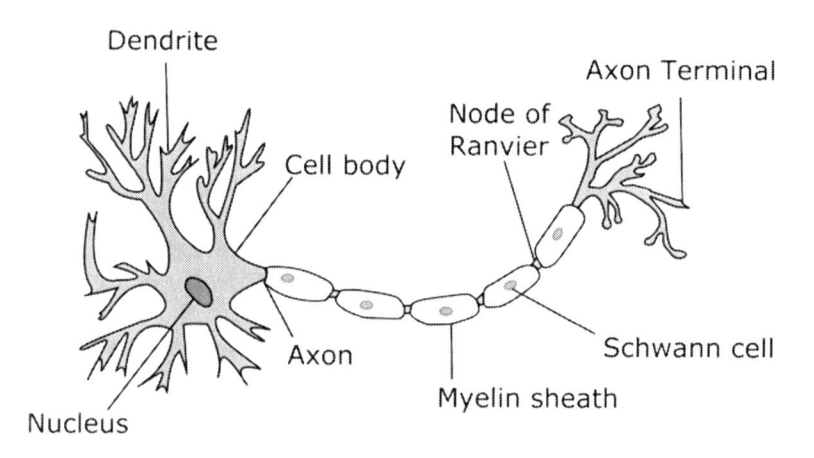

Gate Theory - The brain can process only one sensation from each part of the body at a time. This is the phenomenon behind cold spray, *Ben Gay*, *Tiger Balm*, etc. Neurons from the skin get to the brain faster than those from the muscle underneath. Thus, when you apply a cream that "burns/freezes," that sensation blocks the pain sensation from coming through. However, it is important to note that these creams do nothing to heal you, only block the pain from that area.

Neurotransmitters - Neurotransmitters are the chemicals released by one cell that affect another cell. The receiving cell has special receptors on the surface, to which these chemicals bind. Several illegal drugs act by binding to these receptors, thus changing the circuits in your brain. **Dopamine** and **serotonin** are two important neurotransmitters that help to regulate mood, aggression, sleep cycles, temperature, etc. This is why these illegal drugs often cause people to have such wide mood swings. Other psychological issues, such as **Bipolar Disorder,** also have to do with an imbalance of these chemicals. It could also be that the chemical concentrations are fine, but there is a missing or unexpressed gene for one of the receptors.

There is also some evidence that as martial arts training improves mood and provides overall stability in life, it can also help even out the balance of neurotransmitters to more normal levels.

Sympathetic Nervous System - The Sympathetic nervous system is the part of your nervous system that is activated in the "Fight or Flight" response. These nerves hit the major organs in your body which are responsible for priming it for action. This includes increasing your heart rate, stopping digestion, dumping adrenaline in the blood, etc. This is also activated a few seconds before you wake up. This system will make you ready to compete or defend yourself.

As martial artists, it is important to train ourselves to not only recognize our "fight or flight" response, but **to act effectively throughout the system changes**. The sympathetic nervous system activates in response to being startled or in an unfamiliar or scary situation. Imagine walking by yourself at dusk and a large noise startles you from behind. Adrenaline dumps into your system and your pupils dilate, preparing you to deal with a possibly dangerous situation. A rabid dog, thief, or sexual predator could have sprung out from a bush and be heading towards you.

Properly dealing with adrenaline dumps is a benefit that martial arts should provide to every student. Most martial arts schools already provide a gradual way to deal with this through "simulated pressure." Most promotion tests are not strictly necessary in terms of determining whether or not the student knows the material. The real value to the student comes in terms of making her perform under an adrenaline dump, which will give her experience in a real life self defense situation. The same could be said for the value of competitions.

Lesson 40: Immune System

The immune system is a critically important part of your body. It is responsible for keeping your body safe from infections caused by other organisms. When something dies, it is completely taken over by bacteria, fungi, etc. and decomposes in a matter of weeks. This is what the immune system is constantly fighting against.

Skin – The skin is the first line of defense. When skin is intact, it does a great job of not letting infectious materials through. The problem usually comes when the skin is cut or punctured. This is why proper bandaging is especially important for martial artists.

Lymph System – The lymph system is like the circulatory system, but the lymph fluid is basically just the blood plasma. The lymph system is also responsible for sweeping up bacteria and viruses and bringing them to the **lymph nodes**. Swollen lymph nodes are often signs that your body is fighting an infection. The lymph system will bring the infectious agent to the lymph nodes where the body can fight it.

Thymus – The thymus is an organ near your heart which is responsible for producing **T-Cells**.

Spleen – The spleen filters blood coming through, removing old and damaged blood cells as well as infectious material. People without a spleen will get sick much more frequently than people with an intact spleen.

How pathogens infect cells
All viruses and bacteria have specific markers on their coats that "say" what they are. These markers interact with receptors on the cell membranes, causing the cell to take the pathogen inside where it can cause damage and replicate itself.

Antigens

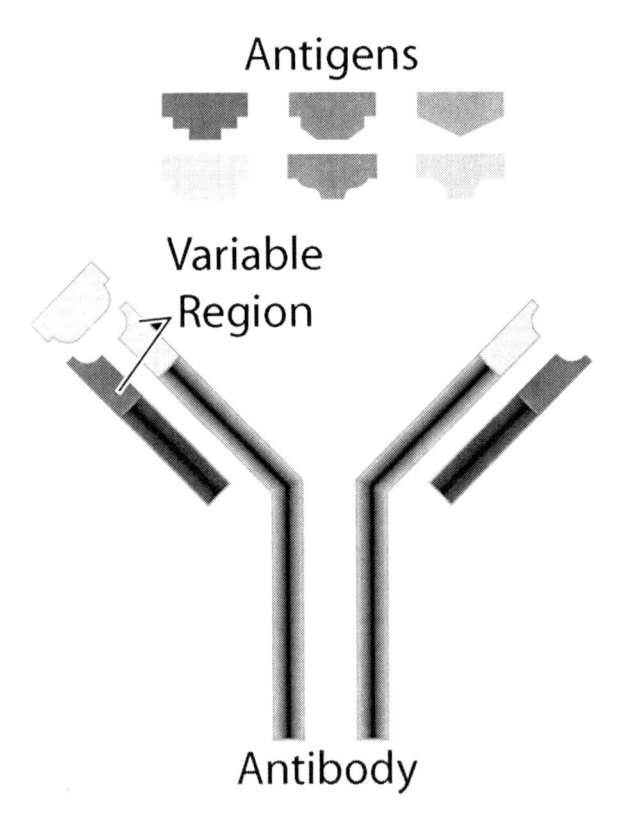

Variable Region

Antibody

Antibodies – **Antibodies** are Y shaped molecules you produce that are specific for each **Antigen** (Antibody Generator.) An antigen could be the marker on the pathogen's coat that says what it is. These antigens bind and gum up the receptors, so that the pathogens can't enter the cells. Also, the antibodies send signals to other cells to come and destroy the tied up invader. One of the interesting things is that antibodies can be transferred to confer immunity. For instance, breast milk can help keep a baby safe from things the mother's body knows how to fight against.

Teaching Martial Arts

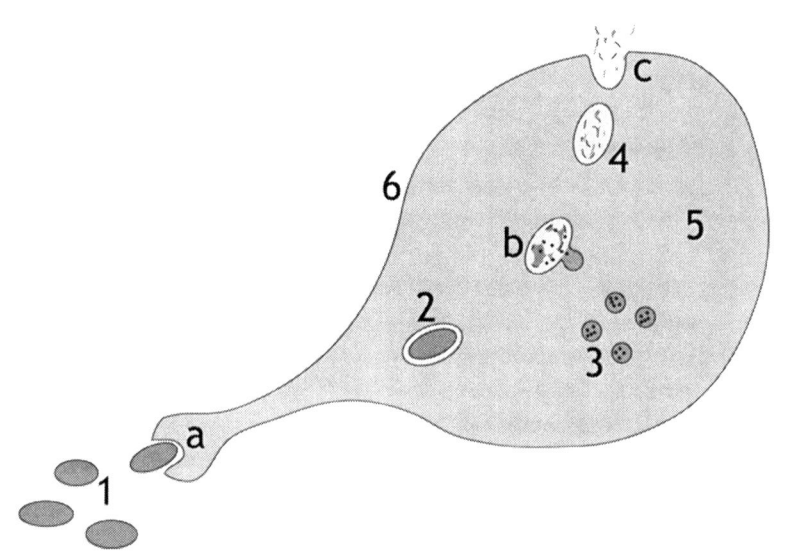

The figure above depicts a macrophage engulfing a foreign body.

Macrophages – Literally means "big eaters." The **macrophages** come to clean up the mess. They launch out tentacles and engulf foreign bodies. Later, they release enzymes that break the foreign bodies down. Macrophages are a type of white blood cell.

Lymphocytes – Two other critical lymph cells are **B and T lymphocytes**, named based on whether they mature in the **bone marrow** or the **thymus**. The B cells produce antibodies. Thus, for every possible infection you've received, there are some B cells floating around. You might have Chicken Pox B cells, e. coli B cells, Salmonella B cells, etc. When a B cell detects an infection, it gets to work copying itself millions of times. Those millions of cells each release millions of antibodies into the blood.

One of the main types of T cells is the **Killer T Cell**. These cells find your body's cells that have already been compromised by a virus or bacteria. The virus will hijack the machinery in the cell and start using that cell as a virus factory. The Killer T cells find compromised cells and destroy them.

Major Histicompatibility Complex (MHC) – We know how the immune system recognizes specific antigens, but what about when it comes upon a new agent it's never seen before? That's where the MHC comes in. Each person has their own unique MHC. It's also known as a 'self' marker. It's on every cell in your body.

This can be a big problem when trying to help the body, especially in transplants. If you get a new heart, your immune system will see that there are different MHC and will reject the new tissue.

Training in general makes the immune system stronger, and many people who train regularly are rarely sick. However, while good general health will help prevent many diseases, there are some diseases that it can do nothing against. Understanding the basics of the immune system is important for martial artists so that we know not to train when too sick and not to let our students train when too sick either. Studying the way the body fights invaders can also give you insight into the nature of combat between two groups.

Lesson 41: Muscle System

To start off the muscle system we will begin a little bit more technical and then move onto the martial arts interpretation. Muscles take inputs from the nervous system and then cause body motion. Muscles (and how to control and strengthen them) are of incredible importance to martial artists. We will focus on **skeletal muscles** as opposed to **smooth muscles** (stomach, blood vessel walls, etc.).

Muscles are incredibly diverse in form and function. Every skeletal muscle consists of muscle tissue, vascular or blood tissue, connective tissue, nerve tissue and several nuclei. Skeletal muscle fibers are single muscle cells that are cylindrical in shape. A muscle is made up of hundreds or thousands of muscle fibers that are connected together by connective tissue. Muscles have a large supply of nerves and blood vessels for contraction.

Contraction is the main function of muscles. Essentially, how you move, flex, grab, throw, kick, punch, etc. are all due to muscle contraction. Skeletal muscle looks banded because of the layout of protein filaments (**myofilaments**) called **actin** and **myosin**. The actin myofilaments slide over the myosin myofilaments contracting the muscle (reducing the size of what is called the H Band). During relaxation of the muscles, the myofilaments slide apart again. The contraction and relaxation of each muscle fiber takes energy which is a finite resource within the body at any given time. A martial artist must be attuned to their own body to understand their health levels and what their bodies are capable of.

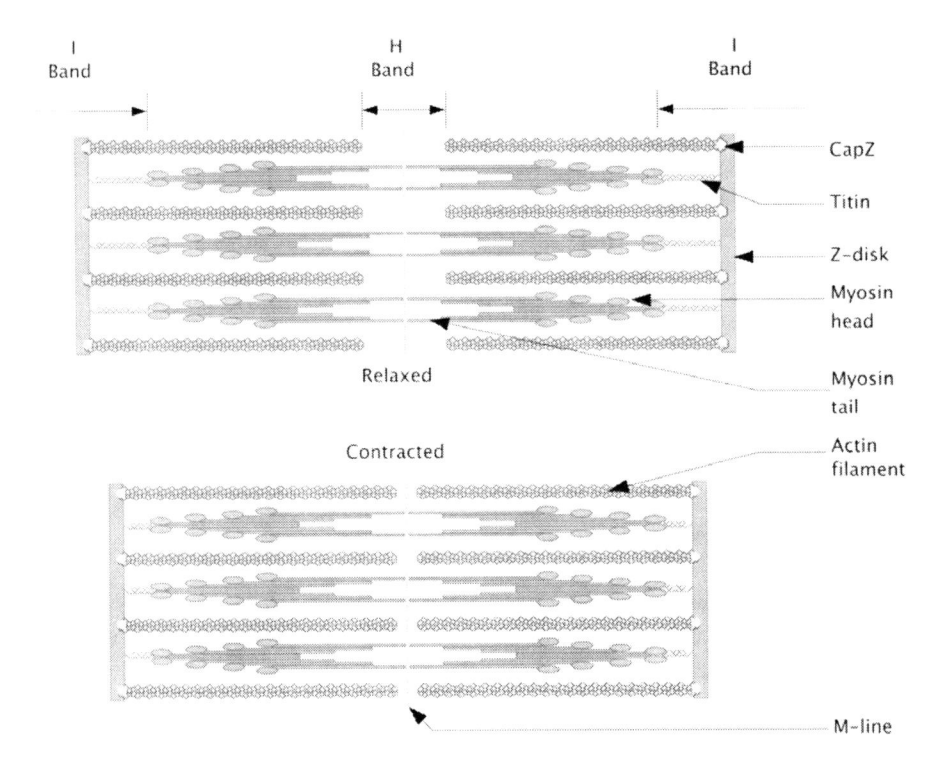

Musculature fatigue is actual, physical fatigue. At this point your muscles have used up all available energy, and the waste byproducts of the muscles working such as **lactic acid** have built up to the point where the muscles doing any further work is inefficient and/or ineffective. No more muscular work can be done beyond this point, and any attempt to push beyond this point could result in serious injury. The important thing to understand is that the more physically fit a person is the longer musculature fatigue will be delayed per each workout.

Before getting into how to build appropriate muscles in a good way, it is important to understand pain and how it pertains to muscle growth and injury. Pain in the form of soreness is common a day or so after an intense workout or even a common workout if someone is not in excellent shape. This type of pain is good as opposed to a sharp or chronic pain which could indicate injury or un-mended damage. Regular soreness after a heavy workout is both natural and an indication of muscle building. Microtears are the main cause of natural soreness; the healing process not only repairs the muscle, but builds the muscle in the process. Note that excessive workouts causing too many microtears will not build muscle faster, but damage the muscle and keep it from fully healing or building.

Now to think on what types of muscles you want to be building and how to focus your efforts to build each type of muscles. There are slow-twitch and fast-twitch muscle fibers; each is important for every type of martial artist; however, the ratios of developed fibers will be different in each muscle depending on the specialization of that individual. **Slow-twitch muscle fibers** have a well developed blood-supply and are able to contract and relax slowly for extended periods of time. These types of muscle fibers are developed through aerobic respiration training and are good for martial art areas such as: forms (poomsae/katas), endurance sections of sparring rounds, basic training, etc. In contrast, **fast-twitch muscle fibers** do not have a good blood supply, but are wonderful for explosive bursts used in areas such as: exchanges in sparring matches, any type of fast and powerful striking, jumping, tricking, etc. These types of muscle fibers can be built up through anaerobic exercise. Moreover, basic fast-twitch muscle fibers can be converted to **fatigue resistant fast-twitch** through careful training – giving the best of both worlds to strong sparring and tricking competitors.

Lesson 42: Combining Forms

Oftentimes when looking at medical words, things seem more complicated than they are. For instance Arthritis comes from Arthro (joint) and –itis (inflammation) so it literally means "Inflammation of the Joint." Study the following relevant terms to be able to decipher anatomical instructions.

When teaching this lesson, you may want to spread it out over several weeks or teach one letter's worth with each anatomy lesson.

The following is a partial list from Wikipedia.

A

Prefix/Suffix	Meaning
a-, an-	not, without, less
ab	away from
acous/acouso-	hearing
acr/acro-	extremity, topmost
–ad	toward, in the direction of
ad-	increase, adherence, motion toward, very
adip/adipo-	fat
–aemia	blood condition
aer/aero-	air, gas
aesthesio-	sensation
–al	pertaining to
alge/algesi-	pain
ambi-	around, on all sides, both
an-	not, without
angi-	blood vessel
ante-	before

140

anti-	against, opposed to
arteri/arterio-	artery
arthr/arthro-	joint, articulation
–ary	pertaining to
–ase	enzyme
–asthenia	weakness
–ation	process
auri-	ears (aural)
aut/auto-	self, same

B

bi-	twice, double
bio-	life
blast/blasto-	germ or bud
brachi/brachio-	arm
brady-	slow
bucc/bucco-	cheek

C

carcin/carcino-	cancer
cardi/cardio-	heart,
cephal/cephalo-	head
chem/chemo-	chemistry, drug
chlor/chloro-	green
chondrio/chondro-	cartilage, gristle, granule, granular
chrom/chromato-	color
–cidal/cide	killing, destroying
circum-	around

cis-	on this side
co-, com-	with, together, in association
contra	against
costo	ribs
crani/cranio-	cranium, skull
cry/cryo-	cold
cycl-	circle, cycle
cyst/cysti/cysto-	bladder or sac
cyt/cyto-	cell

D

dactyl/dactylo-	digit (finger or toe)
de-	away from, cessation
derm/dermis/dermato-	skin
–desis	binding
dextr/dextro-	right, on the right side
dis-	separation, taking apart
dynamo-	force, energy
–dynia	pain
dys-	bad, difficult

E

–eal	pertaining to
ec-	out, away
ect-	outer, outside
–ectomy	excision, removal
–emia	blood condition
–encephal/encephalo-	brain

endo-	internal
epi-	upon
erythr/erythro-	red
eu-	good, well
ex-	out of, away from
Exo-	exterior, outward
extra-	outside

F

fibr/fibro-	fiber
–form	in the form or shape of

G

–galact/galacto-	milk
–gen	origin or production
gloss/glosso-	tongue
gluco-	glucose
glyco-	sugar
–gram, graph	recording
gyn/gyno- gynae/gynaeco- gyne/gyneco-	woman

H

hem/hema/hemat/hemato-	blood
hemi-	one-half
hepat/hepatico/hepato-	liver
hidr/hidro-	sweat

hist/histio/histo-	tissue
hydr/hydro-	water
hyper-	above normal, excessive
hypo-	below normal, deficient

I

–ia/iasis	condition
–iatrics	treatment
–ic	pertaining to
–icle	small
–ics	organized knowledge
idio-	self, one's own
infra-	below
inter-	between, among
intra-	within
irid/irido-	iris
–ism	condition, disease
iso-	equal, like
–ist	one who specializes in
–ite	the nature of, resembling
–itis	inflammation
–ium	structure, tissue

K

karyo-	nucleus
kerat/kerato-	cornea
kin/kine/kinesi/kinesio-	Movement

L

lacrim/lacrimo-	tear
lact/lacti/lacto-	milk
laryng/laryngo-	larynx
–lepsis/lepsy	seizure
lepto-	light, slender
leuk/leuko-	white
linguo-	tongue
lip/lipo-	fat
lith/litho-	stone
log-	speech
–logist	one who specializes in study
logo-	speech
–logy	study of
lymph/lympho-	lymph
lys-/lyso-/ -lytic	dissolution

M

macr/macro-	large, long
mast/masto-	breast
meg/mega-	large
melan/melano-	black
mes/meso-	middle
–meter	instrument for measuring
–metry	process of measuring
micr/micro-	smallness, one-millionth
mon/mono-	single

morph/morpho-	form, shape
muscul/musculo-	muscle
my/myo-	muscle
myc/myco-	fungus
myel/myelo-	bone marrow
myring/myringo-	eardrum
myx/myxo-	mucus

N

necr/necro-	death
neo-	new
nephr/nephro-	kidney
neur/neuri/neuro-	nerve
normo-	normal

O

oculo-	eye
odont/odonto-	tooth
odyn/odyno-	pain
–oid	resemblance to
olig/oligo-	few, little
–oma, onco-	tumor
oo-	egg, ovary
oophor/oophoro-	ovary
ophthalm/ophthalmo-	eye
orchi/orchido/orchio-	testis
orth/ortho-	straight, normal, correct
–osis	a condition, disease or increase

ost/oste/osteo-	bone
ot/oto-	ear
–ous	pertaining to
ovari/ovario/ovi/ovo-	ovary

P

pachy-	thick
pan/pant/panto-	all, entire
para-	alongside of, abnormal
path/patho-	disease
pelv/pelvi/pelvo-	hip bone
–penia	deficiency
per-	through
peri-	around, about
–pexy	fixation
–phage/phagia	eating, devouring
pharmaco-	drug, medicine
–phil/philia	attraction for
phob/phobo-	exaggerated fear, sensitivity
phon/phono-	sound
phot/photo-	light
–plasia	formation, development
plasty	surgical repair, reconstruction
–plegia	paralysis
pneum/pneuma-	air, lung
pod/podo-	foot
–poiesis	production
poly-	multiplicity

por/poro-	pore, pourous
post-	after, behind, posterior
pre-	anterior, before
pro-	before, forward
psych/psyche/psycho-	mind
pyo-	pus
pyro-	<u>fever</u>

Q

quadr/quadri-	four

R

radio-	radiation, radius
re-	again, backward
rect/recto-	rectum
ren/reno-	kidney
retro-	backward, behind
rhin/rhino-	nose
–rrhaphy	surgical suturing
–rrhea	flowing, discharge
–rrhexis	rupture

S

salping/salpingo-	tube
sarco-	flesh
schiz/schizo-	split
scler/sclero-	hardness
scoli/scolio-	twisted
–scope	instrument for viewing

semi-	one-half, partly
sial/sialo-	saliva,
sinistr/sinistro-	left
–stasis	stop, stand
–staxis	dripping, trickling
steno-	narrowness, constriction
stheno-	strength, force, power
stom/stoma-	mouth
sub-	beneath
supra-	above, excessive
sym-	together

T

tachy-	fast
–tension/–tensive	pressure (of blood)
therm/thermo-	heat
thorac/thoracico/thoraco-	chest, thorax
thromb/thrombo-	blood clot
–tic	pertaining to
–tomy	cutting operation
tono-	tone, tension, pressure
–tony	tension
tox/toxi/toxico/toxo-	toxin, poison
trans-	across, through, beyond
tympan/tympano-	eardrum

U

–ula/ule	small

ultra-	beyond, excessive
uni-	one
ur/uro-	urine

V

varic/varico-	swollen or twisted vein
vas-/vaso-	duct, blood vessel
vasculo-	blood vessel

X

xanth/xantho-	yellow, yellowish

Y

–y	condition or process of

Z

zo/zoo-	animal, animal life

Lesson 43: Curriculum Design

The curriculum, or what you teach, is at the heart of any martial arts school. It goes without saying that each instructor must have a thorough knowledge of every move (at least, at or below his own level.) There is just no getting around that statement. **Anything less and you're not teaching, you're distributing errors throughout the school.**

However, it's usually beyond the scope of individual instructors to set the curriculum for the school. Even some head instructors might not feel comfortable doing it, since the curriculum has been set for many years, often by their own instructor. Even so, it is still the head instructor or school owner's responsibility. Ideally, belt curriculum shouldn't be changed, but in reality, martial arts changes. Changing belt requirements should only be done after great thought and planning. Here are a couple of notes about curriculum design:

- **Curriculum** can refer to everything you teach at your school, while **belt curriculum** refers to what is required for each belt. For instance, you might teach back flips to the demo team, but you're not going to require them on a belt test.
- Some parts of non-belt curriculum can and should be changed easily and often.
- Belt curriculum should be meticulously documented (videos preferred) and distributed to the students.
- Curriculum shouldn't *look* over or underbearing. If a new student sees five pages of requirements for white belts, it may turn them off.
- Teach white belts not to look for 100% improvement overnight, but 1% a day. Teach white belts to be in it for the long haul.

The main point of curriculum and even the entire belt system is to keep students externally motivated until they can achieve internal motivation. Therein lies the difficulty. How do you give something that's simple enough for a 5 year old white belt, yet still challenges a 13 year old black belt who has 3 years to work before their next test?

Most schools have a roughly even amount of material to learn at each belt, yet at those same schools, a student will go from white to yellow much faster than from red to black. This is slightly ameliorated by the fact that requirements are usually cumulative since the day a student started. A better way is to have an even amount of curriculum per time. For instance, if it's 2 months from white to yellow and 1 year from 1st black belt to 2nd, the requirements for the latter should be six times as much as the former.

Different schools also have different philosophies about the age of the student and the meaning of the belt. In our school, we don't agree with that. A 6 year old green belt knows exactly what a 40 year old green belt knows. They would both do the same board break, although due to size the child would break a much smaller and thinner board made specially for children. Physical feats are also the same. Thus a women testing for black belt would spar three women, a child spar three children, and a man spar three men. One way we augment this for very small children by giving them more steps, thus they earn intermediate belts that no other students earn.

A key lesson can be learned by looking at long fantasy-type video games, for instance, the *Final Fantasy* series by Square Enix. The games have a certain plot objective, i.e., 'defeat the dark force and save the world.' Players with less time, motivation, or patience can go directly to the main evildoer. However, there are also crossroads on the way to the boss's lair, where other players can spend time exploring and earning rare, powerful, and unnecessary items.

What does this have to do with martial arts? The key is that some of the "sidequests" are significantly longer and more involved than the main quest. Defeating some optional monsters might be 100 times more difficult than defeating the main bad guy. The game designers have found a way for some people to enjoy the game for 50 hours, while others are still challenged for 250 hours.

Try to set up "sidequests" in your curriculum. The main quest is the belt system, but give plenty of optional opportunities that are much more difficult for your best and most motivated students. This could include competition teams, demonstration teams, special patches or awards, optional forms and techniques, special mountain or survival training, extra weapons, etc. Some of the "sidequests" should be significantly more difficult than getting a black belt. This will keep top students motivated, without daunting less motivated students.

Lesson 44: Basic Business Concepts

Signing Up Students - Dealing with prospective students is usually the job of the business manager. Although following the guidelines in this book will be very good for business, this is not a business textbook. There will be times when it will fall to an instructor to meet a prospective student and give them information about the school. Keep in mind the following tips:

- **Ask them questions** – Whoever is asking the questions controls the outcome of the conversation. Ask the students or the parents questions to figure out what they are looking for, then explain to them how your school can help them, or not. Most schools have several different programs. Knowing what they are looking for can help you tell them what will most benefit them.

- **Benefits, not features** – While you will have to tell them what the schedule is, when they can come to class, etc., remember that it is your job to explain the benefits of training. People want to know how training will help them.

- **Get their Information** – Make sure to write down their name, phone number, and how they heard of the school. Don't forget to also write down what they are looking for! Your school should have some type of form for this. If not, just write it on a piece of paper and give it to your supervisor.

- **Good First Impression** – You know the saying about how many chances you get to make a first impression. Make sure everything about you and the school is professional and great. The students walking in will get a different feeling from you.

Service Recovery - Service recovery covers a time when something went wrong (whether it was your fault or not) and you have to go above and beyond to fix it. This is very important, because we invest so much time and energy in each individual student, we don't want to lose them if it can be prevented. There are two key parts to a service recovery. First, **fix the problem**, and second, **take action to make sure it doesn't happen again**.

A common service recovery might go something like "*My daughter is getting really frustrated because she still hasn't learned her form.*" Now, you might have gone over the form several times, but she didn't attend class on those days. Whatever the case, offer to stay a few minutes after class and work with her or give a free private lesson (fix the problem) and then remind them about the time when you work on requirements (so that it won't happen again).

Although most of the ordering/scheduling/etc. will be taken care of by the school owner or head instructor, you still might run into a situation. Perhaps you recommended someone get shoes and they asked you to order some, but you forgot. You could make sure they come quickly, and offer to pay the difference in shipping to get it overnight. Oftentimes, in a case like this, the person would tell you to not worry about it. However, they will still be happy that you went out of your way. That is the important thing— you should go out of your way to try to make it up to them. They will be impressed with the effort that you make, especially if you are very busy.

Remember, we always want to give the students more than they expect. We want them to feel as if they are taking advantage of us. That way, they will be more likely to recommend their friends to come and train. Oftentimes, after a service recovery, the customer is *more loyal* than if nothing had happened at all.

Lesson 45: Coaching at Tournaments

This lesson is presented as a supplement because many schools do not compete in tournaments. If you have followed the lessons in this guide and worked hard, you should have prepared your students well. However, there are several important tips that can help you when it is time to participate in tournaments.

- **Choose your tournaments wisely** – Even if you aren't in charge of the tournament, parents and students will associate what happens at the tournament with martial arts in general and possibly even with your school in particular. Make sure they receive a good value for their money. You can never ensure that everything will go well (even when you run the tournament) but make sure you are putting them in an environment that is safe.

- **Register early** – Some tournaments will let you register on the day of competition, while others will charge hefty registration and coaching fees, even a week before the tournament. Registering early can help you know who will be competing and who will decide not to at the last minute.

- **Divide coaching responsibilities** – There are several ways to divide coaching responsibilities. For small schools, you will likely just coach all the students. For larger schools, you can divide the students beforehand by giving each coach a set of specific students to coach (either by names or all kids, black belts, etc.) Another option is to set each coach to a ring and just have that coach work with whoever comes through that ring. Alternatively, you could have one coach work with warming up the students, one wait with them, and one be in the chair. However, it is good for one coach to spend as much time with the students as possible.

- **Be a calming influence** – Often students will need you emotionally more than they will need you technically. Especially if it is their first competition, sometimes they just need you to calm them down and let them know that they just have to do the same thing that they do in practice every day.

- **Be prepared** – If the tournament is different from what you normally do, check into gear requirements, rules, and bracketing/scheduling procedures.

- **Tournament kit** – We bring a tournament kit with a video camera, tape, extra mouthpieces, cold packs, and kicking paddles to each competition. Each coach has one, because students will often forget required equipment. Parents will thank you for thinking ahead, as someone will almost always forget something.

- **Coaching style** – Some coaches will get really excited, while some prefer to always remain calm in order to keep their player calm. Find your own style and stick to it. It is important to advocate for your players, but remember that you are a martial artist first! Before you throw the chair at what might have been a terrible call (the referees are almost always volunteers) think about how this will look to your students who are sitting in the stands.

- **Sleep and food** – Give your students recommendations on which foods to eat at the tournament, and make sure that they have tried them at practice first. Remind them to get a good night's sleep 2 nights before, because they probably won't sleep well the night before, no matter what they do.

Lesson 46: Basic Physics of Martial Arts

Sometimes the phrase 'martial art' can be misleading, since in the modern area there has been more of an emphasis on science than art. Certainly, the art aspect is still very important in martial arts. However, science tends to dig to a deeper level. One can appreciate the work of an artist without knowing exactly how the artist has put together his creation. With science, we search out the fundamental natural principles. For example, one might say *"That is a beautiful kick"* and appreciate the movement. The scientist would ask *"What specific things about that kick make it beautiful?"* and then when he discovers them, think how he can apply what he has learned towards making other kicks beautiful in the same way.

It is important to study physics in order to understand the basis behind martial arts techniques. It is important to study math in order to understand physics. One important kind of math to study is calculus. Although it sounds difficult, there are two main important concepts to learn.

The derivative- $\partial y/\partial x$ **-** The derivative is just a fancy way of looking at how something changes with respect to something else. So, the above equation is basically just saying the change in y divided by the change in x. Often time (t) is substituted for x. For example, the change in position divided by the change in time is known as velocity, or speed.

The Integral- $\int y$ – The integral is the opposite of the derivative. It usually has limits applied to the top and bottom of the $\int$ and it is basically saying to add up the small contributions of some part to the whole over those limits. It's also known as the 'area under the curve.' For example, to find your body mass, you'd take the integral over the shape of your body of the contribution of each infinitesimally small area of your body. Basically, add up the mass of every cell in your body to find the total mass.

Now that we got the calculus out of the way, let's go on to some basic physical quantities.

- **Mass [kg]** = The weight of an object divided by gravity.

- **Force [n]** = The ability to move a mass.

- **Energy [j]** = The ability to do work
- **Position [m]** = The location of an object

Notice that the letter in brackets [] states how each quantity is measured. Mass is in **kilograms**, force is in **Newtons**, energy is in **Joules**, and position is in **meters**. Most of the names of units come from famous scientists.

We must be careful here because in martial arts we often think of someone as having a forceful kick. But we usually don't mean this in the same way physicists mean it.

Let's see what happens when we start applying derivatives to those four fundamental concepts. Let's start with position.

First let's see how something's position changes with time, $\partial P/\partial t$. As stated above, we see that this is the object's velocity. An important thing to note about velocity, however, is that it is a vector so it has two components, magnitude and direction. Thus, something can change its velocity by speeding up or slowing down, or by going at the same speed in a different direction.

- **Velocity [m/s]** = Change in position over time. $V=\partial P/\partial t$

Now what happens if we take the derivative again? Acceleration is the term for how fast something's velocity changes. Again, this can be a change in magnitude or direction. Acceleration is a key component in martial arts. If someone is fast, but fast all the time, then the opponent will be able to time them. If someone can change their speed or direction quickly, then they will be very difficult to beat.

- **Acceleration [m/s²]** = Change in velocity over time. $A=\partial V/\partial t$

In order to find an object's velocity, we can integrate the acceleration over time. We can integrate again (the velocity) to find an object's position.

If we do the same thing with energy, we find that the change in energy with respect to time is called Power. But the change in energy is also referred to the as Work, so we get two definitions for Power.

- **Power [j/s or w]** = Change in Energy over time. **P=∂E/∂t**

Power is measured in Watts where one Watt equals one Joule/second.

But what do we mean when we say that someone's kick is powerful? We need a few more concepts to explain what happens when someone strikes another person. There are two critical things that happen- **a transfer of momentum** and **a transfer and dissipation of energy.**

The first important concept in collisions is called momentum. Momentum is what is transferred from one body to another when they run into each other. The other important thing to note is that **Momentum is always conserved**. This means that all of the Momentum transferred from one body is absorbed by the other body.

- **Momentum [kg m/s]** = Mass times velocity m*v

In a collision, we have that the Force equals the change in Momentum divided by the change in time, or **F=∂M/∂t.** This leads us to the second important concept, called Impulse. The Impulse is simply the Momentum delivered in a specific time.

- **Impulse [kg m/s^2]** = Momentum delivered in a specific time. **M*∂V/∂t**

As you can see from above, ∂V/∂t is really Acceleration, so this can also be stated as F=MA. In fact, this is known as Newton's Second Law. All Momentum is delivered only if the two bodies are allowed to remain in contact for an infinite amount of time. For our purposes, when hitting another person, we have only a short amount of time in which to transfer our momentum.

The next critical point is that of the transfer and dissipation of energy. There are many different kinds of energy. You have potential energy due to gravity and the chemical bonds in your body. You have energy stored in your muscles like a spring. But the most important for Taekwondo is your Kinetic Energy. This is just a fancy way of saying that you foot has energy because it is in motion.

- **Kinetic Energy [j]** = Energy of a moving object $(\frac{1}{2})mv^2$

Just like momentum, **Energy is conserved**. It may change forms, sometimes to unusable forms like heat and sound, but it will not be totally lost.

What happens when one person strikes another?

There are two main kinds of kicks, **pushing kicks** and **snapping kicks**. Pushing kicks include linear kicks like cut kick, and front kick and back kick can also be done in a pushing way. Even roundhouse kick can be done to push, although this is rare. In pushing kicks, the main purpose is to move the other person's body. Thus, the main equation is F=MA. You are trying to apply a Force in order to cause the other person's body to undergo an Acceleration. What happens if the other person is big? M will be large and then that will make A small. This just proves what you already know, that if you kick a bigger person they will not go as far as a smaller person kicked the same way. However, because of the concept of impulse, if you are in contact with the person for a shorter time (lower t) there will be a larger change in (MV). Thus, hitting for a shorter time will let you move someone farther.

Pushing kicks are not done to score, and the main scoring kicks are snapping kicks. In these kicks you are transferring momentum to the opponent and also transferring energy. Here the physics term Power comes in as the amount of Energy we can transfer in a specific time. Energy transfer is what is really important in snapping kicks, especially roundhouse kick. When your foot is in contact with a person, the Kinetic Energy from your foot is transferred to their chest protector. Some of this energy is transferred to heat energy, some is transferred to sound energy, and some penetrates into their body. Energy is the physical force that is responsible for causing damage, not Force or Momentum. Energy is also the physical quantity responsible for breaking boards.

In a kick like a back kick, momentum transfer plays a larger role. In this case if the opponent is coming in, the change in momentum is greater because you add together the momentum of his body and the momentum of your kick.

But what does this all tell us? First of all, from the Kinetic Energy equation we see that the Velocity term is squared. So Velocity has a much bigger effect on Energy transferred that mass. Say you increased the mass three times. The kinetic energy would increase by three times. But if you increased the Velocity by three times, the Kinetic Energy would increase by 9 (3^2) times!

This helps explain why people with long legs seem to be able to score so much easier. We didn't state it before, but the Velocity in that equation is the Instantaneous Linear Velocity. That means the speed that the foot is going right at the moment that it hits the chest pad, in the direction going into the chest pad. Your leg can be considered like the radius of a circle that is swept out in your roundhouse kick. Angular Velocity is how fast something goes around in a circle. Your entire leg is moving with the same Angular Velocity, or else it would fall apart. But in order for this to be true, the tip of your leg has to be moving with a faster *Linear Velocity* than your knee. Thus, you will transfer more energy by hitting someone with the tip of your leg, and the longer your leg, the more energy you will be able to transfer.

Q: How does this apply to attacking with a weapon?
A: You will be able to transfer more energy by hitting with the tip of a weapon or with a longer sword or staff.

So where does the quantity of Force come in? Force is more of a steady state quantity, thus it is of more use to us in grappling. There are two key concepts we need to learn about.

Have you ever seen someone lie on a bed of nails and not get hurt? Why do we slap the ground on our falling techniques? The answer to these questions lies in the concept of Pressure. Pressure is simply the Force applied divided by the Area over which that Force is applied.

- **Pressure [Pa = N/m^2]** = Pressure equals Force divided by Area.

Pressure is what really causes impact injuries. When being stabbed by a knife, the Area is extremely small (only the knife point that touches your skin) so the Pressure is large. When a person lies on a bed of nails, the total surface area is the sum of the area of each small nail point. Thus the total pressure is not large enough to cause the nails to puncture the skin. When we do the falling techniques, we lower the Pressure by increasing the Area in contact with the ground.

The next concept is called Torque. Torque is what causes rotation. Torque is extremely useful in trying to flip an opponent or in applying most joint locks. Torque is sometimes referred to as leverage, and it is the product of the magnitude of the Force and the distance away from the rotational point.

- **Torque [NM]** = Torque equals Force times Distance.

For instance, say you are applying a joint lock on the thumb. Say you press at the near side of the thumb nail, 1 cm from the joint. Then say you instead press at the far end of the thumb nail, 2 cm from the joint. By only moving one centimeter away, you have effectively *doubled* the Torque on the joint and doubled the pain of your opponent.

The best way to cause rotation is to apply two forces such that they add together and both put Torque around the part of the body you want to rotate. Two forces acting in opposite directions is called a **Couple.** This is extremely important when trying to trip or sweep an opponent. Try to 'sweep' someone by putting your leg behind their leg and pushing on their shoulder, and then try the same thing while sweeping with your leg and pushing on their shoulder at the same time. Also, the farther both forces are from the point about which you are rotating, the larger the Torque. This is why it can sometimes be easier to trip tall people, or why you are more stable in grappling when you spread out to a low and wide base.

This talk of tripping leads us to the next important concept, Balance. In order to be balanced, the integral (sum) of all the forces acting on your body must resolve to a vector that passes through some point on your body that is on the ground. Sound complicated? It's not. It merely says that if you lean one part of your body in a certain direction, in order to be stable you must lean another equal part in the opposite direction. Thus, when doing a side kick, your chest leans back while your foot protrudes outwards. When doing a spin hook kick, your chest leans down and away from the kick to counterbalance your leg.

Angular Momentum and Spinning Kicks

Angular Momentum (the tendency for something to keep spinning) is an important concept for spinning kicks. Angular Momentum is also conserved as long as no forces act on the system. This means that your rate of rotation multiplied by your moment of inertia about the axis which you are spinning will be constant. Or, in another way, your shape determines how fast you spin.

The moment of inertia is the integral of each part of your body times the distance away from the axis you are spinning on. So, the farther your body parts are from your rotation axis, the larger your moment of inertia, and the slower you will spin. You've all seen ice skaters who start with their arms out (high moment of inertia) and then slowly move their arms in (low moment of inertia). What happens? They start spinning faster.

How can we apply these concepts to martial arts? Well, remember the importance of acceleration. Thus, you can change your speed quickly by starting with your arms and legs far out and then once you start a spin you can tuck them in quickly to get an extra boost. For instance, from open stance say you throw a butterfly kick with your legs and arms out. Your opponent will think that they have time to counter with their back leg roundhouse kick. But, at the last moment you bring your arms and legs close to your center and with the extra spinning velocity launch a back kick right into the unsuspecting player's chest.

This concept is critical for doing advanced demo kicks like 540s and 720s. If you start the kick with your arms wide or legs spread, you can 'store up' extra spinning power that you will be able to call upon at the apex of your jump.

These concepts might seem difficult, but if you take the time to study them you will see that they are merely a more thorough way of describing things that you already know.

Class Planning Worksheet

Use the following worksheet to help plan out your classes to make sure that things run smoothly and everything is where it needs to be.

Date: _____
Name: _____

Activity	Time (mins)	Items Needed	Notes

Class Report

Use the following report to make notes about your classes to keep for future reference.

Name:

Class date/description: (I.e., Monday 5/23 beginners' class):

Students attending:

What went particularly well? Why?

What could have gone better?

List any follow up to be done later (I.e., Check Johnny's form next week, order a new t-shirt for Billy, etc.)

The Misadventures of Master Malo is meant to be used in the full course for the examinations for level 1, 2, and 3. It is given here as a supplement to the material presented above. Go through each part and try to find what Master Malo does that you could do in a different and better way!

The Misadventures of Master Malo: Class

It's a beautiful sunny day outside. The autumn leaves are beginning to fall and the apple cider is beginning to flow in the distinctive way that only happens in Anytown, USA. Master Malo pulls up his car in the dojang parking lot right at 4:30 and gets out of his car, still talking animatedly with his girlfriend on his cell phone.

He walks up to the door where several students and parents are waiting to be let in. He fumbles with the keys and then gets the door open. "Yeah," he agrees. "Last night was awesome. The part I likes best was when you…" the rest of his conversation is drowned out as the students rush past him and onto the floor. They begin to play tag and hit each other with kicking paddles. Master Malo watches them a few minutes while bringing in and opening the mail. "Yeah, get him, Johnny!" He cheers as one student whacks another. "That'll teach him to be such a wuss!"

The kids continue to play as Master Malo finally wraps up his conversation. "Well, I gotta go. I have a 4:30 class with the wiener kids again." Master Malo goes into the locker room and reaches into his bag for his uniform. It's wrinkled and still wet from the night before, and his belt is nowhere to be found. It's too much effort. He just changes into his sweat pants and keeps on his *Budweiser sponsors Spring Break in Cancun* t-shirt.

It's 4:40 by the time he bows in the class. Mentally, he goes back and forth in his head what to teach. He finally just decided to see how the class feels and go with the flow. "Okay," he says, looking at the kids. The lines are uneven and belts are tied incorrectly. They're just kids. He can't expect too much from them. "I guess everyone's warmed up. Let's start with some paddle drills. Everyone go get kicking paddles and a partner." He pauses while the kids go get their paddles and line up.

"The first combo is my favorite one. Everyone start with high roundhouse, then spin hook, and then 360 spin hook. Do it 50 times." That should give him some time to think. If only his head didn't hurt so much. He really didn't see why they could send a man to the moon but they couldn't find a cure for a simple hangover. Some of the black belts were doing the technique well, but a few of the white belts were looking confused. He went over to one of them.

"Hey, white belt. You've got to turn your hips into it. What are you trying to kick, a smurf?" Master Malo goes to hold the paddle a bit higher. The white belt kicks up, and then writhes on the floor in pain. Master Malo bends to examine it. "It looks like you might have pulled your leg. That's why it's really important for you to stretch before class."

A green belt raises his hand from the middle of the line. "Sir, what can I do to make this better." Master Malo sighs. This kid has no talent. "I don't know… why don't you try… not sucking?"

Just then, the door opens and another student enters the class late. "Hey, Bobby," Master Malo shouts, inclining his head toward the new student. "You need to show respect for the class and get here on time. Give me 100 pushups."

"Yes, sir." Bobby hits the floor and starts working.

Master Malo looks around at the class again and sees that they aren't making progress right away. "Okay, time. You guys are hopeless. Let's move on to something else."

The class stands there while Master Malo thinks for a minute. "Hmmm… no… well… I know. Let's do some forms. It's time for Kyukpa!"

The class all lines back up again, except the white belt who is sitting on the side of the floor still in visible pain.

"I guess we better start with Chun-ji," Master Malo states. "Okay everyone, first move, back stance, down block! Make sure you have your weight evenly distributed on each leg in back stance. That will keep you from falling over."

The door opens again and a smoking hot girl enters and looks around. Some days, Master Malo wished he could afford to hire a receptionist, but today isn't one of them. "Freddie," he says, pointing to a black belt in the first row. "You take over for the rest of chun-ji while I go help this woman out."

"Yes, sir!" Freddie responds. He's only 12, but pretty good at teaching.

Master Malo saunters over to the lady and puts his hand on the wall next to her head. "So," he says, making sure his delivery is perfect. "How you doin?"

"Uh… pretty good," she replies. "I have a 5 year old son and I was thinking about signing him up for tai chi or Taekwondo."

"Well," Master Malo replies "Tai chi is just for wussies. Your son's not a wussie, is he?"

"Well, he's only five," the mother responds, starting to squirm with the invasion of her personal space.

"That's okay, don't worry about it. You've come to the right place. I'm an expert at Taekwondo. We can give your kid confidence, weight loss, discipline, and all those good things."

"That's great," says the mom. "I heard it can also help him concentrate and do better in school."

Master Malo shrugs his shoulders. "Sure, whatever you want. The important thing is that we respect all our students." As he's speaking, something catches Master Malo out of the corner of his eye. He turns to yell at one of the students. "Hey, yellow belt, you call that a crane stance? Maybe some ugly, lopsided crane with a broken leg that keeps falling over all the time. You're never going to learn chun-ji."

The woman takes another look around the training area. The parents look bored or disinterested. She notes that the only smile in the place is the creepy one on Master Malo's face that's really starting to weird her out.

"I was wondering something," Master Malo starts. "Was your father a mechanic? 'Cause I was wondering how you got such a finely tuned body."

"Um.... I'm not sure this is the right school for us," she manages to get out.

Master Malo shrugs again. "Eh, it doesn't matter. Anyway, can I get your number? We should head out for drinks sometime."

Despite his Master-like reflexes, the woman is out the door before he can even blink.

Back to the class, Master Malo runs them through a few more drills, but his heart isn't in it. He puts a handwritten sign on the door to cancel the rest of the classes for the day, and heads back home to sleep for a few hours before he goes out again.

Master Malo and The Promotion Test

It's the middle of the summer, and once again time for the school's promotion test. Master Malo is excited for the test. He has a big trip to Vegas planned for after the test, and his plane leaves in 3 hours. With rent, equipment purchases, and whatever else he's been spending his money on in the school lately, he's managed to get a bit behind. If he can just make double or triple the money he earns from the test, he'll be able to finally pay back the electric bill.

Master Malo comes out of his office. His uniform is clean, but he probably should have taken a shower or maybe even shaved. He's got the head table set up, and only one of the guest masters he invited has shown up. It doesn't matter. Master Malo is a highly trained professional. He could run the entire test by himself, blindfolded.

"Alright, students," Malo calls out in a commanding voice. Line up to pay your promotion test fees." The students trickle over with crumpled bills in their hands. Malo takes Jimmy's fee, and Johnny is next. All Malo's students have stock names like that, or at least they do in his mind, as he frequently has trouble remembering their names until they become high belts.

"Sir, can I pay with a credit card?" Johnny says, holding out a piece of plastic.

"What?" Malo answers, caught off guard. "I can't use your credit card in Vegas!"

"Excuse me?!" Johnny's mom flashes him a dirty look.

"Uh…" Malo is quick to recover. "I said, 'I can't use your card for today's test.' Our credit card machine is still broken."

"Well, I don't have any cash on me. Do I have time to get it before the test starts?"

Malo nodds. "Sure, no problem."

A few more students come by and then it's Jimmy2, a white belt who just joined a few weeks ago. "Master Malo, am I ready to take the test?"

"Did you bring your test fee?" Malo asks.

"Yes, sir."

"Then you're ready! You've been working really hard for this and gaining a lot of confidence and whatever."

Jimmy2's face brightens, but he is still a little apprehensive.

Malo takes the rest of the students' fees himself, noting down how much each pays on a sheet of paper. The students have long ago learned never to ask for receipts.

Malo bows the test in and lets one of his black belts start the warmup while he reviews the requirements that he's jotted down in his notebook. He looks out over the test and the audience to see if any of the three hot moms managed to show up. Not one of them or their kids made it to the test. Malo hoped that this bad luck wouldn't carry over to Vegas. Come to think of it, though, he wasn't sure the last time he had seen Jasmine, Katy, or Samantha (he had no trouble remembering *their* names) come to watch their kids. Well, the test isn't a total loss as there is one attractive girl whom he's never seen before. He makes a mental note to go over to her later.

After a few minutes he thinks he's got the curriculum down, so he lines the test up and gets started with everyone. He leads them through some of the white belt requirements, but soon it's apparent that the higher ranks have forgotten their basics. The guest master looks uncomfortable, embarrassed for Master Malo. Malo quickly orders the color belts to have a seat and continues on with the white belts.

"Okay, everyone sparring stance and show me twenty crane kicks."

The white belts stare forward, bewildered. Malo's not amused. "Come on guys, crane kicks. Don't you remember last week when I had to leave early so I put on *Karate Kid* to teach you?"

There are some flickers of recognition in a few of their eyes, and then a few terrible crane kicks follow. Johnny2 is completely out of sync.

Malo glances at his watch. He has to hurry this test along to make it in time for his flight. He bows the white belts out and brings up the rest of the test as one group. As they're lining up, he hastily scribbles "PASS" on all the forms so he can concentrate on the curriculum.

Alright, yellow belts do combination 17, green belts combo 14. The green belts fire it off, but the yellow belts look around without a clue. Malo looks down at the curriculum and rifles through the sheets, trying to see what the yellow belts should know. "Oh yeah," he corrects himself "combo 5."

The test continues in this way for about an hour longer, Malo calling up the groups one by one. The test is small, and he finishes in plenty of time to go and hit on that hot girl.

Malo saunters over to the woman and gets ready to unleash a great line on her, but before he can, another woman who Malo didn't notice before cuts in front. "Hi, my name is Cheryl." Malo looks her up and down for the first time. She's not unattractive, but pretty overweight. Cheryl points to the good looking woman. "This is my sister, Katrina."

Master Malo looks Katrina up and down. "You know, if I had a nickel for every time I saw someone as beautiful as you, I'd have five cents."

Katrina tries to pretend she didn't hear the comment, and Cheryl continues "Bradley is in my class at school and always talks about how much he likes Taekwondo, and I heard it has a lot of benefits."

"Oh yeah," Master Malo agrees. "Taekwondo definitely will help you with your problem of being too fat."

Katrina grabs Cheryl by the elbow to take her out. "I don't think this is the right guy to teach us."

"What?" Master Malo complains. "You don't think I'm one of those Mr. Miyagi, wise old sensei types? How about this:

You may fall from the sky
You may fall from a tree
But the best way to fall...
Is in love with me!

As soon as they are gone, a mom of one of the white belt girls comes up. "So, how did my daughter do on the test? Did she pass?"

Master Malo fingers the wad of money in his pocket. It's a little lighter than he would have liked. "Well, she did *pretty well*... but there are many factors that go into whether someone passes or not. A little *extra contribution* to the school certainly never hurt anyone's chances."

The mom is visibly upset. "Are you asking for a bribe?"

"No, no," Master Malo responds quickly, but the rest of his conversation is cut off as Johnny's mom comes up to him complaining about how she left to get cash for the test fee, and missed Johnny's test. Malo can't take it anymore, and his plane is about to leave anyway. He grabs his keys, runs outside, and jumps in his car to race away.

Master Malo Goes to the Tournament

Master Malo pulls his car up into the parking lot at the local high school where the tournament is scheduled. Man, 9:30 is early for a Saturday morning! He's glad that he cancelled Saturday morning classes a few years ago. Malo shifts the car into park and then twists the key in the ignition and pulls it out. He steps out into the cool spring air and locks the door behind him. Malo is reminiscing about all the tournaments he used to compete in. He'd do anything to get his conditioning and technique back where it was when he was younger. Well, anything but train, that is. He certainly didn't have time for that!

He follows the signs and soon reaches the registration booth. A couple of his students are standing in the long line marked 'late registrations.' Malo wishes the tournament entry forms hadn't been lost in the pile on his desk for so long. Then his students could have sent them in ahead of time. Fortunately, Malo's best student Freddie is almost to the front of the line, so Malo cuts ahead of everyone else to walk up to him.

"Hi Sir," Freddie says. "I'm feeling really great today!"

"Awesome," Malo responds, but he isn't really listening. His old nemesis, Master Meticulous, just came in with paddles to warm up his son. That guy was always working so hard. He was probably trying to make everyone else feel bad. He was probably still mad about the time he and Master Malo had been training together. Master Malo had been older by two years and a black belt at the time. Master Meticulous had been a yellow belt who just entered sparring class. Master Malo had gotten him pretty good, and then pretended to be hurt after Master Meticulous had become a black belt and wanted to spar. Come to think of it, that gave him an idea.

"How are you doing, sir?" Master Malo shook hands with his nemesis. "Got any good students here today?"

"I'm doing well, sir." Master Meticulous replied. "All of my students are working hard and getting better. And my son finally decided to join. He's a yellow belt and this is his first tournament."

Master Malo couldn't believe his luck. "Excellent! Well good luck to him and I'll see you guys in there."

They finally get to the front of the line and Freddy starts writing down his information on the application. Master Malo steps forward to help him with it.

"I know this form is a little hard since you're *just starting*," Malo picks up a pen. "But here under rank that's where you put "yellow belt."" Malo gives Freddy a creepy wink. Freddy knows not to question his instructor in public, so he goes along with it. Later his parents take Malo aside.

"Our son is a black belt," Freddy's mom says, a little agitated.

"Of course he is," Malo agrees. "But you don't know these tournaments like I do. All the other instructors cheat. They give their black belts yellow belts and their yellow belts black belts. Then they have their yellow belts go into the black belt division and lose by getting disqualified for illegal hits. Then their real black belts win the color belt divisions. I'm just keeping him safe." Master Malo smiles. He's pretty impressed with himself that he was able to make that up on the fly.

Freddy's parents have never been to a tournament before, so they can't argue. They head in to go get warmed up while Malo goes to the admissions table.

"That will be $5," the woman manning the table says. Malo fumbles in his pockets before realizing he forgot to pick up his coach pass from the registration table. No worries. If there's one thing he's learned from watching all those James Bond movies, it's that all problems can somehow be solved by making out with beautiful women.

Teaching Martial Arts

"I'm Master Malo and I registered to coach today, but forgot my pass over there. However, I want to make sure this tournament is safe first. Did you guys hire a fireman? Because your body is smokin' hot!"

The woman looks at him, not sure whether to laugh or cry. "Uh... just go... please."

Malo pumps his fist in the air. Yes! He still had it.

Malo walks in to see that the forms divisions are all already under way. Freddy comes up to him, a little nervous. "Sir, I missed my forms because the yellow belts already finished."

Malo shrugs it off. "Don't worry about it. Forms are for wussies. You're not a wussy, are you?"

"No, sir!"

"Good, now go and warm up for your sparring. And, you might as well warm the other students up as well."

"Yes, sir!"

Master Malo looks around at all the rings, seeing how the tournament is going. Some kids are doing well. It will be a tough day for his students. At least he only brought.... Well, he's not exactly sure which of his students ended up signing up. He's pretty sure it's not more than 5 or 6, though.

Master Malo walks by the medical stand and almost gets whiplash. The EMT woman standing there is much prettier than the one taking the tickets. It takes him only a fraction of a second to come up with the perfect line.

"Excuse me," he says, putting his hand down on the table next to her. "Do you have a band-aid?"

"Sure," she says, reaching down to get one with a smile. "What do you need it for?"

"I think I scraped my knee falling for you."

The silence is palpable.

The woman looks like she's not quite sure how to respond, and then suddenly a real injury comes in. The woman looks almost relieved. "Uh... that's .... nice. Well, gotta go. Duty calls!"

Rejected but not deterred, Master Malo heads to the stands to check out the action. A couple of times his students or their parents come up to ask him something about what pads they need or when their forms are starting or something like that. Master Malo isn't really sure because he's only thinking about the hot EMT girl and whom to blame for the fact that his students aren't as successful Master Meticulous's.

Soon it's time for Freddie's match, and Master Malo gets the first good news of the day. Freddie has drawn Master Meticulous's son in the first round.

Master Malo heads to the ring to give Freddie a pep talk.

"I can't believe that guy has the audacity to smile over there after everything he said about your mom."

Freddie is confused. "I didn't think he even knew my mom. What did he say?"

"I certainly can't repeat it here!" Master Malo smiles to himself. That one worked every time.

Their discussion is cut short as the referee comes in to call the competitors into the ring. Master Malo looks across from him and stares down Master Meticulous.

The match begins with Master Meticulous's son George attacking sloppily and Freddie easily countering to earn a few points. It's clear that the two are at much different skill levels.

"Yeah!" Master Malo cheers. "Now go for the head!"

Freddie switches feet and does a medium contact roundhouse to George's head, which is scored by the judges.

"Harder!" Master Malo yells. "What are you waiting for?!"

Freddie attacks again, this time hitting a little too hard. He immediately receives a penalty point.

"Come on, ref!" Master Malo gets up, visibly agitated. "Is this Taekwondo or Ballet?"

The ref turns and issues a warning to Master Malo, at which point he just rolls his eyes back in disgust. Finally, the round is over, with Freddie up 14-0.

Freddie comes back to the chair, but Master Malo is not there. Freddie looks around for a second before he sees Master Malo crawling around on the floor, searching for something next to one of the corner judges.

"Excuse me," he asks the judge. "Do you have your phone number? I seem to have lost mine."

Soon the break is over, and the corner judge has not said a word to Master Malo. Master Meticulous's son has a gash over his eye and has decided not to come back for the second round. Freddie is declared the winner, but does not seem excited. He is eyeing the black belt divisions, where he knows he belongs.

Master Malo sees that Freddie isn't too pleased and feels bad. "Don't worry about it, kid, it's been a tough day for all of us. Tell you what. Let's get out of here and head to a bar. I'll even buy you a beer." See, he wasn't such a bad guy after all.

Sample Certification Requirements

For more information and details see martial-arts-instructor-training.com.

Level I: Junior Instructor

Requirements
- At least high red belt
- Be age 13 and above
- Pass quizzes on lessons 1-27
- Assist a total of 20 classes
- Earn CPR and First Aid Certification
- Pass a physical exam.
- Pass the Level I test with 70% or above.

Level II: Instructor

Requirements
- At least 1st degree black belt
- Be age 16 and above.
- Pass quizzes on lessons 28-42
- Assist a total of 50 classes
- Pass a physical exam.
- Pass the Level II test with 80% or above.
- Show development during on the job performance

Level III: Senior Instructor

Requirements
- At least 4th degree black belt
- Be age 20 and above.
- Pass quizzes on lessons 43-46
- Teach a total of 200 classes.
- Pass an elite physical exam.
- Pass the Level III test with 90% or above.

- On the job performance is the main requirement to pass to level III.

The US Armed Forces publish guidelines for standard physical tests. Level I and II could pass regular tests, while level III would have to pass an elite (Navy SEALS, etc.) test.

References

There are a number of excellent books and resources available for martial arts teachers.

www.wikidrills.com – A comprehensive site filled with many different martial arts drills.

National Association of Professional Martial Artists (NAPMA) – A trade association that publishes *Martial Arts Professional Magazine* and is connected with the Mile High Karate Franchise. http://www.napma.com/

Martial Arts Industry Association (MAIA) – Another trade association that is owned by Century Martial Arts. They publish the *maSuccess* magazine and sponsor the yearly Supershow conference. http://www.masuccess.com/

Kovar's Sartori Academy – Master Dave Kovar's *Martial Arts Career Training* was one of the first texts on instructor development.

American Council on Martial Arts – They have a great manual on teaching and an independent certification program.

Teaching Martial Arts: The Way of the Master: Great book written by Dr. Sang Kim

Fighting Science: Good introduction to martial arts physics by Martina Sprague.